WEST KIRBY

An RAF National Se...

To:

DENNIS TOMLINSON

Happy memories !
— Dennis Tomlinson
Feb. 6, 02

Dedicated to John and Gladys Bernstein
who made life more pleasant for 30,000 West Kirby erks

Entrance to RAF West Kirby
Photo copyright RAF Museum. Reference P4517

AMELIEL PRESS

West Kirby and Beyond
First Published 2001 by

Ameliel Press
66 Greenborough Road
Sprowston
Norwich NR7 9HJ

ISBN 0 9534505 2 X

Typeset & printed by Catton Print of Norwich

Contents

Cover Illustration:
Harry Dodd's drawing, used on the cover of West Kirby Parade
(the station magazine), is a 'before and after' of a recruit's eight weeks' training.

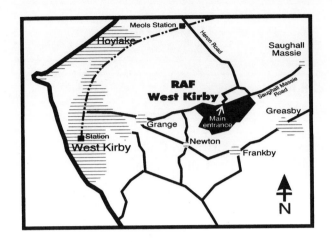

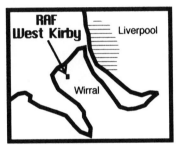

Acknowledgments

Many people have helped with providing the stories and photographs without which this book could not have been written. I am grateful to them all. References to historical events have been checked but if you find something that was not as you recall it at West Kirby, please remember that many things changed over the years and memories are sometimes at fault. The following organisations have been especially helpful: Public Record Office; RAF Museum; Air Historical Branch, Ministry of Defence; Birkenhead and West Kirby Libraries; Unilever Historical Archives; friends at the Methodist Church, Westbourne Road, West Kirby; Norfolk County Library Service; Eastern Counties Newspapers Library; Daily Telegraph; Mirror Group Newspapers; Western Morning News. For help with research, I am indebted to The Dean of Liverpool; Jill Bonell; Peter Cannon; Robin Godfrey; Jim O'Neill; Phil Newman and Jim Simpson. For technical assistance, David Button; for maps and drawings, Kevin Cole. As honorary proof-readers and pickers-up of errors I thank my wife Grace (whose patience has never been exhausted), Ray Church and Andy Duncan.

Introduction

EXACTLY 50 years after starting my National Service in the RAF, I decided to write my memoirs of those momentous two years. Momentous because they were the first time I had lived away from home, the first time I had been to the North of England and the first time I had been subject to strict discipline since leaving school.

I left West Kirby in May 1950 and had not been back since. So, where to begin? I wrote a letter to the Liverpool Echo which was published on January 29, 2000. In it I asked if anyone remembered two girls who I had known at the Methodist Church at Westbourne Road, West Kirby. They used to help entertain young recruits who went to evening service; one was named Jean - she recited a poem about the DIs (Divine Instructors in her language). The other, whose name I couldn't remember, sang; I remembered her singing "One Fine Day" from Madam Butterfly.

These two scraps of information put me in touch with Gladys Bernstein, widow of the youth club leader who had organised the Sunday evening entertainments. Gladys, 86 at that time, was still writing regularly to both girls - Jean, in Canada, and Jill, the singer, in Australia. Jill phoned me from Australia and said: "I am the little blonde girl you remember singing at West Kirby."

I was also put in touch with Ada Stewart, a former NAAFI girl at West Kirby, who, with Joan Mackay, was organising a reunion at Greasby on April 1. I went to the reunion, visited the old camp site and then obtained a list of 150 former West Kirby recruits from Robin Godfrey who had been at the camp in 1954. I wrote to them all. Many replied, some with photographs, and the best of their stories appear in this book.

It has been a long trail - journeys to the Public Record Office at Kew, countless telephone calls and letters to museums, archives and individuals. But it has produced a record I believe to be unique, which includes the first history of RAF West Kirby to be published. Read on - you may find an old billet mate somewhere within the pages.

Ada Stewart, right, and Joan Mackay, organisers of the 2000 reunion, pictured on the camp site.

Christmas Call-up

CHRISTMAS DAY 1949 - and a brown envelope marked OHMS (On His Majesty's Service) dropped through the letterbox at my home in White Waltham, Berkshire. Yes, letters were still delivered on Christmas Day at that time. My letter told me to report to High Wycombe for a medical exam, that my fares would be refunded and that if I was to be called up for military service, I should receive at least 14 days notice.

I went for the medical, was weighed, measured, sight-tested and had my reflexes tested. I passed Grade One. I also did an aptitude test involving shapes and patterns and was tested for colour-blindness - essential if you had ambitions to fly. Interestingly, my eye colour was recorded as brown; when I was demobbed two years later it was given as blue. The actual colour is hazel. So much for colour-blindness tests.

I was also asked to nominate six RAF trades I would like to be considered for. I chose clerk General Duties (shorthand typist); operations clerk; fighter plotter; teleprinter operator; motor cyclist. I chose the last trade on the advice of my elder brother Brian, a wartime dispatch rider in the Royal Signals. He said: 'If they won't give you one of the other trades, you can at least enjoy yourself riding round the countryside.'

Motor cycling ran in the family - my brother John had been dispatch rider in the village Home Guard platoon and did his two years 'hostilities only' service in the Fleet Air Arm from 1945-47. In choosing the RAF, I made sure all three services were represented in our family.

My summons to report to RAF Padgate on February 16, 1950, duly arrived, complete with rail warrant. I gave notice to my employer, the editor of the Maidenhead Advertiser, where I had been working as a trainee reporter since leaving school. The editor had told a former trainee on being called up: 'This will make a man of you, Donald.' He gave me no such advice.

In the fortnight before reporting to Padgate, I did a round of farewells to relatives and had a photograph taken by the local portrait photographer: it joined those of my two brothers on the living-room wall.

Entrance to Euston Station in the 1950s - gateway to the North (and Padgate) for thousands of recruits. (Photo courtesy National Railway Museum)

The night before call-up, I went to see the film The Third Man at the Commodore Cinema in Cippenham with my then girl friend, Dorothy. At Paddington Station next day, I asked the way to the Underground from a man who didn't speak English. I found my way to Euston Station and caught the train to Warrington. As we waited for transport to Padgate outside Warrington Station, little pieces of grit in the strong wind that was blowing stung my cheeks. So this was the North!

A three-ton Bedford lorry took us to Padgate, the reception centre for recruits. There, in 1946, a young Bob Monkhouse had painted murals of Mickey Mouse and Popeye on the walls of the station cinema and Betty Grable and Rita Hayworth in the sergeants' mess. On arrival we were given tea and biscuits and a welcome from a flight lieutenant or squadron leader. All very civilised, but things would soon change. Our hair was cut short, we were issued with a 1250 (identity card), given a service number - mine was 2461745- and issued with uniform. We moved in a line through the store and the equipment assistants threw the various items to us in a most un-Grace Brothers manner. No-one asked: 'Are you being served?' Every item had to be marked with our number, using stencils provided.

We were vaccinated against smallpox and the flight sergeant warned us: 'Don't any of you men faint.' We didn't. I had heard horror stories about vaccination; in fact, it

2

was no more than a scratch. At the end of the week, we were allocated to recruit training centres. Mine was West Kirby on the Wirral. Others went to Wilmslow, Bridgnorth, Hednesford or stayed at Padgate. (John F. Hamlin's book, Stand By Yer Beds, gives a list of other National Service recruit training centres).

We travelled to West Kirby by train, locked in the no-corridor carriages so that no one could escape. We had arrived at the camp and it was 5pm before we were allowed to use a toilet. It was a day of acute discomfort for me. On arrival at West Kirby I noticed that the trees leaned inland. It didn't take long to discover why. Strong winds blew frequently during the almost-three months I spent there.

We drew blankets, sheets and pillowcases and were marched (you marched everywhere at West Kirby) to our billets. As I was taller than most of the other recruits, I was made senior man - the only position of authority the RAF ever entrusted to me. I can't remember what the duties were, but there must have been

The author, extreme left, second row, at West Kirby 1950. Centre, front row, Cpl Lavin.

3

some privileges because I never did a guard duty or a fire picket and missed the week of fatigues which most people did.

There were a few damp eyes in the billet on the first night but, although I was living away from home for the first time, I was not affected by homesickness. The station commander, an ex-aircrew group captain, welcomed us next day and told us we were here for eight weeks basic training which would be tough. He also said: 'If you see any man kneeling down to say his prayers in your billet tonight, don't make fun of him. He's probably got more guts than the rest of you put together.' I never saw anyone teased for his religious convictions.

We were not allowed off camp the first weekend. There was one exception; that was if you wished to go to church on Sunday evening. I caught the the double-decker bus provided and went, with others, to Westbourne Road Methodist Church in West Kirby. Strictly speaking, I wasn't a Methodist but I attended a small interdenominational chapel in my home village and put Methodist on my bed card as being the nearest. In 1955, I joined the Methodist Church and have been a member ever since.

The Methodists at West Kirby were very welcoming. Every Sunday night from 1946-57 when there were recruits in the camp, they provided refreshments and entertainment for the lads after the service. As I wrote in the introduction to this book, it was memories of those Sunday evenings which were the first step for me in starting the research for this book. When I returned to West Kirby for the reunion in 2000, I went to the church on Sunday morning, received a public welcome from the

Gladys Bernstein with the author. On his lap is her daughter Janet's parrot - Sgt Pepper.

minister, the Rev John Bates, and met several of the former youth club members who had helped serve those refreshments. I also met Gladys Bernstein and her daughter Janet. Gladys's late husband John had started the Sunday evening socials. He had served in the Royal Navy during the war and understood the loneliness of young lads away from home for the first time.

When West Kirby closed as a recruit training centre at the end of 1957, John estimated that

4

30,000 young men had passed through their church on Sunday evenings. Gladys has a collection of 150 letters from ex-recruits, and some from their parents, which I was privileged to see. Among their comments were the following:

Do not really know how to thank you adequately for the wonderful times you gave us each Sunday evening. (SAC Donald Codling, RAF Hospital Halton).

I found in your club, or fellowship, a feeling of friendliness which I have never come across in any other place. (Peter Carton, 22 Reserve Centre, Pucklechurch).

You have no idea what those Sunday evenings meant to me and lots of other lads. (A.G. Merritt, RAF Hospital Weeton).

Jill Coles (nee Griffin) who I had remembered singing One Fine Day on one of those Sunday evenings, contacted me from Australia in February 2000. Her home was in Greasby and she sang with Birkenhead Amateur Operatic Society, playing the female lead (Magnolia) in its 1951 production of Showboat at the Royal Court Theatre in Liverpool. She also sang with The Merrymakers in New Brighton and did a lot of pantomime work. She appeared on the TV show Time for Melody.

Jill met her husband, Hubert Selby, when booked to sing at the Ritz in Birkenhead. He was a cinema organist, originally from Ipswich, and broadcast regularly with the BBC. Eventually they emigrated to Australia where Hubert sadly died from cancer in 1985. Jill has since remarried.

Jill Griffin - 1951

She recalls going to sing at the camp on one occasion and was met at the guardroom by an LAC from the orderly room. On the way to where she was going to sing, Jill said she hoped the RAF had provided a good accompanist as, in the past, some had been awful. Jill takes up the story: 'The young man said nothing but when he accompanied me on the piano he was absolutely brilliant. Afterwards, I felt very small.' She learned that the accompanist was Noel Rawsthorne who was assistant organist at Liverpool Cathedral from 1949-55 and organist at the cathedral from 1955-80. He was senior lecturer in music at St Katherine's College of Education from 1954-93. When I contacted him, Mr Rawsthome remembered the incident well.

Jean Shaw (nee Sly), who recited the poem about camp life and referred to Divine Instructors, met her husband Bernard through the Sunday evening get-togethers at Westbourne Road Methodist Church. Bernard remembers her entertaining with monologues, some of her own composition but including many of Stanley Holloway's masterpieces.

He recalls: 'The only means of getting out of camp legally for the first few weeks was by attending Sunday evening church parade and boarding the special buses to local churches. (We were not considered 'fit to wear the King's uniform in public' - although I am sure the King would never have been caught dead in that rough serge.)

'As the bus paused at each denomination, blue-clad figures would disappear into the dark, some even went into church.' Of an admittedly somewhat loose Methodist affiliation, Bernard dismounted at Westbourne Road, but did not move fast enough to escape. Fortunately, as he recalls, because he met Jean at the youth club. They corresponded while he was serving as a meteorological assistant in Singapore and Hong Kong and were married in 1952.

With two little Shaws (another arrived later) they emigrated to Canada in 1957. Jean continued her career as a physiotherapist and Bernard 'designed bits and pieces for aircraft and rockets,' as he puts it, before joining the federal government's industrial assistance programme and then starting his own consulting business. Both are now retired. Jean sings in an Ottawa choir that performs in local retirement and nursing homes, still getting laughs with monologues like 'Albert and the Lion' and 'The Truth About Men.' She spearheaded a highly successful Millennium pageant celebrating the history of her corner of Ontario. Bernard still does some consulting but devotes most of his time to historical research and has had four books published, the latest on Canadian aerial photography from 1919-39.

But if Sunday evenings at the Methodist Church were pleasant, for the author and his mates it was back to reality on Monday morning and to the DI who once told us we were like a crowd of silly girls. Later batches of recruits went on reliability and initiative training in North Wales. Our biggest test of initiative was to scour the camp to find kindling wood to start the coke stove in the billet. None was issued.

There was just one link with home on the camp. The weapons training officer was Squadron Leader Ted Boyd. My mother had taught him at the village school in White Waltham. He spoke to me and when next home on leave called on my mother to

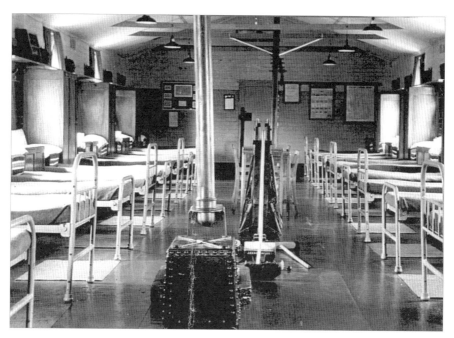

Ready for inspection. Note the gleaming floor of the hut. The beds, possibly hospital type, look more comfortable than those slept in by the author. This photo and the passing out parade (below) are from SAC Malcolm Kirkham, operations clerk, bought during his squarebashing at West Kirby in February-April 1957.

assure her I was being well looked after! I wrote to her every Sunday and my letters, posted at 6pm near the main gate, reached her next morning.

My worst experience at West Kirby was having my first two weeks' pay stolen. I didn't realise it had happened until I got to the NAAFI, opened my wallet and found the £2 was missing. Without being asked, one of the other lads from the billet immediately lent me some money until I could get some cash from home. I never left my wallet on the bed again.

As the date of passing-out parade drew nearer, I was having problems with my boots. Size ten had been too big, so I opted for nines. Unfortunately the left boot rubbed my hammer toe so that it bled and would not heal. I reported sick and was put in the station hospital for five days. I was reflighted (given longer to complete my training). I reported to Cpl Lavin in my new flight and he, to my surprise, treated me quite reasonably. I was issued with an 'excused boots' chit so never wore boots again. On pass-out day I helped empty the dustbins and then kept out of sight. In 1951, an operation at RAF Hospital Halton straightened my toe.

When the postings came up, mine was to No 2 School of Administrative Trades at Hereford; I was to be trained as a clerk GD (shorthand typist) - my first choice of trade. The GD stands for general duties.

(Author's Note: Harry Heywood, whose story appears in Chapter 8, has reminded me of what the senior man's duties were in his time. They included: allocating daily hut duties; responsibility for rifles in the hut when they were not being used for drill or ground combat training periods; care of the PSI (See Glossary) radio in the hut; conduct of airmen from your hut in the dining hall and in the NAAFI. The senior man wore a white armband with a blue stripe on the left arm 'at all times, except when walking out of camp.' He had the help of two deputies.

Harry confirms that the senior man was excused fatigues, was permitted to leave the camp bounds one week after arrival at camp and could be granted one late pass per week until 23.59 hours. George Pettican (see Chapter 5) recalls that each recruit was asked to contribute one shilling (5p) towards the cost of an electric iron on arrival in the billet. The senior man would compile a timetable so that everyone had a turn to press his uniform but George would be called in if an extra keen recruit overshot his time. At the end of the course, the senior man was asked to organise a raffle for the disposal of the iron. George added: 'In most cases, it was beyond further duty. The sole would be discoloured or the flex ragged and burnt.')

2

Back to the Classroom

GOING to Hereford (or RAF Credenhill as it was called in those days) was like entering another world. No DIs, the weather was warmer and the discipline was relaxed. We were there to be trained for a trade and went to the classroom every day to learn about RAF clerical procedures and also how to type. I had attended shorthand and typing classes before call-up, as part of my training as a local newspaper reporter. My three-finger typing did not quite have the rhythm of the beginners who were typing to music. Our instructor was Sgt 'Chalky' White; he came from Aylesbury in Buckinghamshire and was very good-humoured. The class included some regulars, including a flight sergeant, who were retraining from other trades. The whole course reminded me very much of school. Get on with your work and no-one will trouble you was the attitude.

Royal Air Force   Hereford.

No. 2 School of Admin: Trades. No. 1 Wing.

Vivian of Hereford

CLERK GENERAL DUTIES CLASS "A" COURSE No 77 From 1-6-50. To 12-7-50.

AC's Boddy Youden Oliver Smith Everett Jones

AC's Wand Parsons Buttery Naylor Jarrett Tomlinson Mills Plummer

AC's Williams Rae Cpl Jones Sgt White F/Sgt Richardson AC's Phillips Boase

Instructor

9

In my second week test I scored 91.5%. But the work was not easy for those with no clerical background. Several of us gave extra coaching to one young Scots lad who was a regular and finding the going hard. He was surprised to be offered help and delighted when he passed the final tests.

Terrence J. Knight, author of The Fort on the Hill - The Story of Royal Air Force Hereford, has given me permission to quote the following from his book. It gives something of the flavour of the times.

> Secretarial courses expanded in the 1950s, mainly due to the fact that National Service recruits only required a short (usually 6 weeks) training course to fit them for their 2 year stint in uniform and also because the new ground trade structure, introduced in 1951 for RAF career people, demanded specific skills and higher standard as a necessity for promotion.

> The National Servicemen brought their own expertise and characters, for they certainly did not wish to be in uniform and many, especially those who came from the Accounts trade, had left behind careers as Accountants in well-established Companies. It was not unusual for a hut of such National Servicemen to contain airmen with degrees and professional qualifications from all walks of life.

> It is recalled that when one young airman arrived for training, his comment on arrival in the hut was to the effect that he should be treated with respect as he had just qualified as Chartered Accountant. To his dismay, 12 others stated that they were also Chartered Accountants and one of them, who was famous for his bull-nosed Morris, added that they also had their own Practices.

> National Service finished, unfortunately or otherwise, in 1961, and with it vanished the short, intensely concentrated courses in limited trade skills for large numbers of young men who really would have preferred to be doing other things.

(Author's Note: The final call-up of National Servicemen was in November 1960. Some of these were not demobbed until 1963. See Appendix V).

The OD (Other Denominations) chaplain at Hereford was fairly stout, rode a Scott Flying Squirrel motor cycle and told us that when we were choosing a wife, we should select someone with a sense of humour. Several of us went to support him when he took evening services at the village chapel at Kenchester. The chapel was still there when I visited Hereford in the early 1990s.

One Saturday evening, I was strolling along the river bank in Hereford with two pals when we started talking to two girls. They invited us to the Baptist Church in

Leominster the next evening and we went back to the home of one of the girls for a cup of tea. Her father was, I believe, caretaker of the chapel.

We caught the Midland Red double-decker bus back to Hereford and then the bus to Credenhill. My pals had paired off with the two girls. One of them formed a passionate attachment for her young airman; unfortunately, he had a girl friend at home and I don't know which of the two was his final choice. I visited Leominster years later, found the Baptist Church but the area around it had changed greatly.

The slacker discipline on camp had its downside. On one occasion I saw a mess orderly who was sweeping the floor of the mess lift up his broom and sweep the top of the dining table with it. I was also shocked on bull night when someone swept dirt under the linoleum. That would have caused the West Kirby DIs to have apoplexy. One aspect that Hereford did not let up on was haircuts. We were compelled to have a haircut every week - price one shilling (5p). The civilian barber must have made a fortune.

The Hereford camp, opened in 1940, fulfilled many roles for the RAF at different periods in its history. At one time boy entrants were trained there, the RAF School of Catering came there in 1958 and when I visited the area in the 1980s, I was told, rightly or wrongly: 'It's all WAAFs and computers now.' On another visit I saw that Yeoman's Coaches at King's Pyon were still in business. I travelled home on one of their coaches for my 48 (48-hour pass or weekend leave). The RAF finally left the camp at the end of 1994.

During my time at Hereford, I was able to visit my parents once while they were staying with friends at Sutton Coldfield. I took the train to Birmingham, stayed Saturday night in the YMCA and then caught the tram to Sutton Coldfield on Sunday morning. Because I was in uniform, the conductress would not accept the fare - the only time this happened to me. One other memory of Hereford - the notice on the wall of a warrant officer's office (probably the SWO's) which said: 'I can do the impossible immediately but miracles take a little time.'

At the end of my clerical course, I stayed on an extra week at Hereford for shorthand practice. This was usual for potential shorthand-typists who already knew shorthand. I passed out as AC1 (Aircraftman First Class) - a step-up from AC2. My posting was to Northwood - a place I had never heard of. Someone told me there was a Northwood on the Isle of Wight . My Northwood proved to be Headquarters Coastal Command, near Watford - just 25 miles from my home. All things considered, it was a dream posting.

During my training at West Kirby and Hereford, which lasted five months, I came home no fewer than five times - two 48-hour passes, Easter grant, Whitsun grant and five days leave at the end of squarebashing. We even had a day off for the King's official birthday (June 8), having first paraded and given three cheers for His Majesty (Hurrah, not Hooray). This contrasted with my brother Brian who had joined the Royal Signals in November 1940. He came home on leave once, was called back early and then embarked for Egypt. He returned four years and four months later. No wonder my father said to me: 'You're always coming home!'

3

I Flew a Typewriter

I travelled from Hereford to Paddington by train on a warm July day and went to Baker Street to catch the Metropolitan line train to Northwood. It ran through John Betjeman's Metroland. That afternoon, as we travelled further from Baker Street, there were crowds of schoolchildren on the platforms in uniforms of every colour, from the well-endowed private schools along the line. A green London Transport country bus took me the final stage. It stopped outside the camp; the tennis courts were visible from the road. So, here at least, they expected us to have some leisure.

I was within 25 miles of home and, in due course, would have my motor cycle, a 1936 350cc Ariel Red Hunter, on the station and make a prompt getaway for the weekend at 12 noon on Saturday. Before my motor cycle was available, I used public transport and made a complicated journey by bus and Underground to Uxbridge and then, by three more buses, home to White Waltham in Berkshire. Complicated - but cheaper than going via Paddington. Most of the other Command HQs were within similar easy reach of my home - Bomber Command at High Wycombe; Fighter Command at Bentley Priory, Stanmore; Flying Training Command at Shinfield Park, Reading; Transport Command at Bushy Park, Teddington; Maintenance Command at Andover; and Reserve Command at White Waltham - my home village! I did apply for an exchange posting to White Waltham but that was too much to hope for. In practice, I was well settled at Northwood, with just a short attachment to Mount Batten, Plymouth, which I will describe later.

RAF Northwood consisted of a large house - prewar it had been the Eastbury Park Hotel - plus wooden offices and living accommodation, built in the grounds. The big house formed the officers' mess and housed the offices of some senior officers. Because of the high ratio of officers to ordinary airmen

The author's 1936 Ariel Red Hunter 350cc.

13

and airwomen, headwear did not have to be worn, so avoiding the need for unnecessary saluting.

Hot water for washing and bathing in the ablution blocks, was provided from a system fired by a large coke-fired boiler, manned by civilian stokers. No central heating in the billets. We had the familiar circular slow combustion stove in our hut. Billet 40, as the hut was known, had been condemned, so the stove had to be kept going 24 hours a day in winter. George Boulton , who worked on the coal lorry, was in our hut, so we were never short of fuel. Before call-up, George had worked as a van boy for The Star (the London evening paper). The Star, with its companion morning paper the News Chronicle, closed in October 1960. I have often wondered what happened to George after those well-paid and union-protected jobs in Fleet Street vanished in the 1980s.

We were a mixed crowd in Billet 40, mostly National Service in clerical trades with three or four regulars including one older man who had rejoined after wartime service and felt himself out of place with so many youngsters. We nicknamed him Pop.

Billet 40 hutmates at Northwood, June 1951. Left to right, back row: John White, Les Allmey, Les Coombes. Second row: Micky O'Brien, Johnny Cornes (standing), Peter Keable. Third row, George Boulton, Cpl Len Buckley. Front row: Pat Carroll, Don Hanson.

The regulars were paid higher rates than we were (we received the regular rate of pay, an extra three shillings (15p) a day,in our last six months of service). One of the regulars could be noisy when he came back to the billet after lights out. Appeals to make less noise fell on deaf ears so John White and I concocted the minutes of the wholly fictitious 'Billet 40 Less Noise at Night Society.' They were eventually published in the unit magazine, Coastline, and raised a few laughs throughout the camp. Editor of the magazine was Sgt Buckmaster.

Don Hanson, my best mate, had also been at Hereford. Through catching German measles, he missed a posting to Hong Kong at the time the Korean War was starting. Don was an equipment clerk in the stores and often went back to his office in the evening to work on the correspondence course he was taking for his Chartered Institute of Insurance examinations. He eventually became the youngest Fellow of the Institute in his company, the Liverpool, London and Globe. His diligence inspired me to see the education officer when a new textbook for journalists, The Kemsley Manual of Journalism, was published. The education officer obtained a copy for me to borrow and I was so fascinated by this book that I read its 400 or so pages in the evenings of one week.

Don came to stay at my home for several weekends and I later visited his home at Batley in West Yorkshire. His father showed me round the woollen mill where he was an overlooker (overseer or foreman in other trades). The mill dealt with the wool in the raw state. It had to be washed, combed and prepared for spinning. I saw lanolin being extracted from sheep's wool.

Don and I once made a day trip from my home to the South coast on my motor cycle, taking in places like Littlehampton, Worthing and Brighton. This was good practice for Don who rode on my pillion seat from Northwood to Liverpool on our way to see the 1951 motor cycle TT races on the Isle of Man. We left the bike with a cousin of Don's mother and took the Isle of Man steamer to Douglas.

We shared a chalet at Douglas Holiday Camp with two strangers. The all-in price was £5 each for the week but the food was so awful that we had to pay for meals elsewhere to stave off hunger. The races were exciting and the Norton team, led by Geoff Duke on a Norton, won the Senior race. We rode over wet cobblestones in Oldham on the way back to Don's home. Fortunately, there was no rain one summer evening when I rode from Northwood to Lewisham in South London with Donald Pye, my fellow personnel clerk, on the pillion seat.The tramlines, which could be a hazard for motor-cyclists, were still in place but we avoided getting the front wheel stuck in them.

A few weeks after arriving at Northwood I was sent on attachment to HQ No 19 Group at Mount Batten, Plymouth, to act as temporary clerk to the AOC (Air Officer Commanding) Air Vice-Marshal G.R.C. Spencer. The Air Vice-Marshal, known as 'Cocky,' could be a fiery character. He summoned officers from elsewhere in the wooden HQ building by banging on his desk and shouting their

surname. He ignored the buzzer provided. But he treated his clerk very reasonably. When he was due to go on holiday for three weeks, he asked me to come to his official residence at Wembury on several mornings to take dictation. I was driven by car and on the final morning the Air Vice-Marshal signed several blank sheets of headed notepaper so that I could type the letters and send them off in his absence. I had signed the Official Secrets Act, so there was no question of my selling secrets to the Russians! This was a concern in those Cold War days. For instance, we were told not to attend Communist meetings in Plymouth.

Coastal Command still had Short Sunderland flying-boats at that time and I was promised a trip in one coming from Pembroke Dock but somehow it never happened. Because of the Korean War and the fear of Russia as a potential aggressor, the RAF brought more airfields back into service. I played a small part in getting RAF St Mawgan reopened by taking a lengthy shorthand note on the telephone from a wing commander who had prepared an inventory of the buildings there, some of which were being used by a local farmer. When we were halfway through the inventory, the wing commander said: 'Would you like a break, Tomlinson?' I said 'Yes' and we both had a breather before completing the task.

I went to church in Plymouth - the Methodist Central Hall. The RAF provided transport at the insistence of an LAC called Jimmy who was a keen Christian. One evening I attended an open-air service to commemorate the sailing of the Pilgrim Fathers from Plymouth in 1620.

When it was time to return to Northwood, the Air Vice-Marshal shook hands and said: 'Come and see me, Tomlinson, if ever you come to Plymouth again.' I am sure he meant it. I did not see him again but, since moving to Norfolk in 1968, I have had a regular reminder of his name. Spencer Road, close to Norwich International Airport (formerly RAF Horsham St Faith) is named after him. As a group captain, he was station commander there early in World War II.

I came back to Northwood in September 1950 and, presumably because of the attachment, my name had been missed off the duty roster. Consequently I did not do a fire picket duty in the guardroom until August Bank Holiday of the following year. That was the only weekend for the remainder of my service that I didn't go home. In summer, providing my motor cycle was available, I didn't go back until Monday morning.

If I left home at 6.30am, I passed the church clock at Iver Heath at 6.50am and was back in camp by 7.20am - in time for breakfast. In colder weather I returned on Sunday evenings and Don Hanson, who could only go home occasionally at weekends, always had my bed made up ready. Except for Sundays, we always had to fold up our bedding and stack it neatly on the bed. Apart from this and the weekly bull night on Mondays, when we cleaned the billet and the ablutions (washroom, toilets etc.), there were no irksome restrictions. We paraded for our pay and I once made the mistake of looking amused when Sgt Price was marching us up and down. I paid the penalty and found myself peeling potatoes in the cookhouse on my 19th birthday!

The work at Northwood was not exciting. Individual records for the whole of Coastal Command were kept in Kardex cabinets - a visible-edge filing system that preceded the computer. If a senior officer came round, it could be 'Stand by your cabinets.' I was kept busy typing draft notes (movement orders) for personnel being moved to other RAF stations. If an RAF police dog handler was to be posted, then the name of the dog went on the draft note too. I distinctly remember a dog called Outlaw. There were often urgent draft notes to be typed just before bank holidays, so while other people were getting early chits and leaving camp at 4pm, I was there until the bitter end.

Our sergeant, Eddie Falconer, was a very reasonable man. If he wanted anything done, he would usually say:'Would you mind, Tommy...'

Because I was a shorthand-typist, I sometimes took dictation from senior officers when their clerks were on leave, notably from Group Captain Taaffe, senior personnel staff officer, and Wing Commander Powell, his deputy. I recall Wing Commander Powell driving in the Monte Carlo Rally. I worked once for the Air Officer Administration, an air commodore, who insisted on having a clean piece of blotting paper on his blotter every morning. He was less than patient the first time I attempted

The hapless airman who backed a car into the AOC-in-C's Humber staff car.

17

to use the three-way phone - something we had not been taught at Hereford. Fortunately, I never worked for another group captain who had a small dog which needed to be taken walkies every morning.

After the changes in the RAF trade structure in 1951, I was eligible for promotion to SAC (senior aircraftman) if I could pass a 100 words per minute shorthand exam and a 40 words a minute typing test. I passed the shorthand but typing was more difficult. I am, to this day, a three-fingered typist and, as the machines we used were mostly Barlocks, to type on one of those with three fingers was little short of a miracle. When I thought I was ready, I told the warrant officer: 'Mr Sanderson, I'm ready to take the typing test now.' He looked up from his desk and said: 'Tomlinson, your typing is all right.' Had I known that a few months earlier, my promotion, and the extra shilling (5p) a day, would have started sooner.

I went regularly to the cinema in Watford and in the run-up to the 1951 general election heard Dr Charles Hill, the Radio Doctor, speak at Watford Town Hall. He was not on the banned political list, so far as the RAF was concerned, and later became a minister in the Conservative government.

There was some attempt to keep us in the picture regarding the threat from Eastern Europe with a talk by a lecturer from the London School of Economics. This was a gentle reminder of why we were doing National Service.

I made use of the tennis courts on camp during the evenings which were available to both ourselves and the WAAFs, whom we greatly outnumbered. Sometimes on sports afternoon, Wednesday, I went with Derek Price to Henley-on-Thames where we took out a skiff. Little did I know that ten years later, my future wife and I would spend the first eight years of married life in that town.

After getting back from sport, we knew without looking what the evening meal would be - sausages. It was only when I discovered that the daily messing rate (the amount of money per person per day allowed for food) was, from memory, one shilling and tenpence (just under ten new pence) that I realised that our rations would stay at a basic level.

We had two county cricketers on the strength who both played for the Coastal Command team and for the RAF and the Combined Services. Both later played for England. Jim Parks (Sussex) described himself as a 'not too efficient LAC pay clerk' who worked in station accounts. His service number was 2500957. Jim played 19 times for the RAF. The RAF played first class games against county sides and Jim scored a century at Worcester in 1952 as part of the RAF's total of over 500.

His cricketing colleague was the Middlesex player Alan Moss, who was serving as an LAC medical orderly in station sick quarters.

A celebrity from a different walk of life was at Northwood after my time. He was 2560678 LAC Richard Briers. In a TV interview in 2000, Richard said that he began acting in the RAF 'but the officers always got the best parts.' He was a clerk (personnel) and confessed 'I was very bored.'

In the last few weeks of my service, we had the most exciting episode of the entire two years. It concerned an American freighter - the Flying Enterprise - which was adrift off Cornwall and was shadowed by Coastal Command aircraft.The crew were taken off but the captain, Kurt Carlsen, insisted on staying on board (see Appendix IV).

So demob came on February 15, 1952 - the day of King George VI's funeral. My release documents said: 'The type of airman it would be desirable to retain in the service.' However, journalism still beckoned and I went back to my job as a reporter on the Maidenhead Advertiser. My pay was approximately £4 a week so financially I was worse off for the next few months until I reached the adult rate of £6 a week. The RAF had been paying me £3.17s (£3.85 in decimal currency) with food, housing and uniform thrown in. I sometimes half toyed with the idea of going into personnel work after leaving the Service, but it was not until 1976 that I found myself in a personnel department as training officer for Eastern Counties Newspapers.

Looking back, I can say that the good times in those two years far outweighed the bad and I echo the view of Tony Thorne, author of Brasso Blanco & Bull who wrote: 'Throughout all of my subsequent life I have enjoyed the Freemasonry that exists between those of us that were fortunate enough to serve as national servicemen.' That has been especially true during the writing of this book.

The kit inspection drawing in this chapter is of the day when an airman at Mount Batten (not the author) told the adjutant that he had 'misplaced his kitbag.' The drawing of the airman backing a car into the AOC-in-C's car at Northwood was an incident that happened one weekend after an unofficial respraying job done for a Wing Commander. Despite an anxious few days for the perpetrator, there was no court martial.

4

'Life in the RAF is not too bad'

2378586 LAC ALICK GRANT, R/T Operator. Alick Grant's links with the RAF began with his call-up for National Service on January 1, 1948. He served for two years which included 15 months working in the control tower at RAF Butterworth in Northern Malaya. He was awarded the General Service Medal.

Alick returned home to Essex and Civvy Street but in March 1950 enlisted in the Royal Auxiliary Air Force. This was the start of more than 30 years as a part-time airman and, subsequently, officer. In March 1957 he enlisted in the RAF Volunteer Reserve as an air defence operator and in 1960 was awarded the Air Efficiency Award. In February 1962, with the disbanding of his unit, he was transferred to the RAF Police and saw service in Germany and Cyprus.

In 1969 he joined 2393 (Billericay) Squadron ATC as an instructor, was commissioned as a pilot officer in the RAFVR (Training Branch) in 1971. He later commanded 2476 (Hutton) Squadron ATC and in 1978 was moved to the East Essex Wing ATC HQ staff. In 1979 he was promoted to squadron leader and eventually retired from uniformed service in 1984 as a wing commander on reaching the age of 55.

Alick Grant's excused boots chit.

Alick kept a diary throughout his time at West Kirby and the following entries are taken from it.

They all relate to the year 1948. Anything in brackets, other than the name of Lime Street Station, has been added by way of explanation.

JANUARY   1 Train Euston to Warrington. Joined the RAF at Padgate.
             3 Vaccination, service number and pay book.
             5 X-ray. Issued with all kit.
             7 Issued with uniform.
             8 Posted to RAF West Kirby.
             9 At West Kirby. Discipline very stiff. Cpls Lobburn, Marr, Tragenza.
          10 Issued with rifles etc.
          14 Photograph taken. Parcel from home.
          15 Pay parade.
          17 Issued with pass. Took Syd's place as mess orderly all day.
          18 Easy day. Life improving.
          19 Life here is still not too good, but seem to be enjoying it better.
          20 Foot started to trouble me. Reported special sick. Light duties.
          22 Started fatigue week. Easy day.
          23 Saw specialist and he reported 'no boots.' Modified course.
          24 Reported sick. Issued with certificate for shoes. Wet weather.
          25 Cookhouse all day. Foot hurts. Haircut by Sandy.
          26 Wet weather. Foot the same. Air Vice-Marshal AOC visited the camp. Lazy day.
          27 Gave up boots, issued with shoes. Parcel from home.
          28 Last day of fatigue week. Fine weather.
          29 Started drill again. Excused OC inspection. Not too good. Wet weather. Pay parade.
          30 Reported sick. Sweet coupons. Fine day.
          31 Easy day. Only six days to 48-hour pass.

FEBRUARY   1 Life here at West Kirby seems a little more cheerful. Easy day. Laid in. Best blue on; fits OK.
            2 Drill again. Wet day.
            3 Wet day. AOC visit. Foot better.
            4 Fired the Sten (gun), 20 rounds. Very busy in evening as we hope to win radio and 48-hour pass. (The best hut won the use of a radio for one week).
            5 Getting ready for 48-hour pass. Got tickets. CTTB (Central Trade Test Board) test - average 79%. (As we had not yet selected trades, I presume they were questions of a general nature to assess our educational standards).

21

6 Left camp at 15.30. Left Liverpool (Lime Street) at 17.25. Arrived Euston 20.00.

7 Up at 08.00. Wet day. Went up the office.

8 Left Euston at 17.20. Good journey. Arrived at camp at 23.59.

9 Hut orderly. Fine day.

10 On range all day. Fired 20 rounds 0.303.

11 Wet day. Busy evening. Life in the RAF is not too bad. Looking forward to seven days leave.

12 Pay parade. CO's inspection of hut. Busy day. Feeling lonely.

14 Told that I was best recruit in flight. Allowed out of camp. Saw Bill in Liverpool. Had a nice day. Went to News Theatre and Littlewoods Cafe. Arrived back at camp at 21.00.

15 Stayed in camp all day. Busy with Blanco and brasses. Burnt hole in best blue. Hair cut. Fine day.

16 Rifle test. Weapon training all pm. Not feeling too well.

17 Dry weather. Feeling better. Drill. Snooker in NAAFI in evening.

18 Busy evening. Only another two weeks to pass out. Now senior flight.

Alick Grant as a young recruit.

19 Inspection. Easy day. Snooker over NAAFI. Sweet coupons.
20 Easy day. Washing from home. Snowing most of day. Very cold.
21 Final kit inspection. Went to Liverpool. Saw Bill. Had photo done at Jerome's. Arrived back at camp at 20.15.
22 Busy all day. Cleaning equipment. Cpl Marr came back. Photo taken with Syd. Rather cold. No snow.
23 Drill and weapon training.
25 Drill. Last bull-night I hope. Very cold.
26 CO's inspection. Very cold. Easy day. Pay parade.
27 Drill. Told officially of Best All Round Recruit Certificate. Cold day. Food situation bad here.
28 Mess orderly. Received photos from Jerome's. Warmer. Confined to camp. Began to get ready for pass out.

MARCH
1 Drill. Mild day. Busy all evening with kit.
2 Drill test. Passed out 85%. Rehearsal. Parcel from home. Busy in evening. Posting and trade.
3 Passing out parade. Presented with Certificate for Best All Round Recruit. Busy day. 'Do' over NAAFI. Getting ready for tomorrow. Pay parade. Issued with warrants. Gave in rifles.
4 Left West Kirby at 09.30 by bus. Left Liverpool (Lime Street) at 11.10. Arrived Euston at 16.15. Pleasant journey. Full kit. Good to be home again.
11 Left King's Cross at 13.25. Arrived at RAF Cranwell (No 1 Radio School) at 17.05

Alick completed training as a radio telephony operator (AC1) with a pass of 61% on June 1, 1948, and was posted to RAF Tangmere.

5

Other People's Stories

FROM the many letters I have received since deciding to write this book, I have selected 50 stories from recruits which tell something of the lighter side as well as the grimmer side of life at West Kirby. In the stories used, the dates in brackets are the dates the individual was at West Kirby. The rank given is the rank achieved after leaving West Kirby.

The DIs (drill instructors) were the bane of our life, having to lick us into shape as smart passing-out material in just eight weeks with a mixture of chivvying, persuasion, threats and sometimes bullying. The language of most, but not all, polluted the skies above the camp. Few of us ever met our DIs again but at the reunion held at Greasby in March 2000, Ken Goatley met his former DI, George Pettican, for the first time since 1950. He reminded George of the evening when he had to take his cap badge to him six times before George was satisfied with its brilliance. Later in the 1950s, recruits received badges which needed no polishing.

4004194 ACTING CPL PETTICAN joined the RAF in 1946 and served for ten years. Originally an equipment assistant, he remustered (changed trades) to the RAF Regiment and went for 12 weeks training at Wombleton - a camp on the Yorkshire Moors, recently vacated by displaced persons, mainly Polish. George recalls: 'The Nissen huts were spread over many acres of moorland, every meal was a 30-minute march. The quality and quantity of food was a disgrace and rapidly reached a climax. One Sunday morning, each man was given a half-slice of fried bread and half a tomato for his breakfast.

'When the orderly officer arrived and asked if there were any complaints, several hundred bods rose to their feet. It

George Pettican in 1951, wearing his first issue of a blue battledress. Prior to this, the RAF Regiment wore khaki with blue shoulder flashes and blue stripes denoting rank.

was the nearest I have been to a mutiny. The orderly officer acted swiftly and put the kitchen staff under close arrest, mainly for their protection, and his own, I think.'

George then went to Catterick for 16 weeks NCO training and arrived at West Kirby in May 1947. After three weeks as a ground combat training school instructor, he was seconded to DI duties with B Squadron, 4 Wing. The CO was Wing Commander Bagshaw. In 1950 George was posted to RAF Buckeburg in Germany and then to Luneberg. This meant relinquishing the acting rank of corporal. Within six months, his stripes were restored and a third added.

The NCOs he remembers who were on drill instruction at West Kirby include WO Dalby, Flt Sgt Wood, Sgt Dodsworth, Cpls Carter, Shipley, Jolliffe, Jones, Cullum, O'Toole and Colby. Cpl Lavin, the author's corporal after reflighting, he remembers as having a sense of humour.

2483472 LAC KEN GOATLEY, batman/waiter, the recruit with whom George was reunited in March 2000, was at West Kirby from August 17 - October 11, 1950. He remembers his first meal on arrival at the reception centre at Padgate. It was kippers and beetroot - said to be very nutritious. Nobody in Ken's family believed that he had been given this meal. But years later, it was confirmed by Tony de Angeli, editor of The Grocer magazine, speaking on Radio 2. He had been a recruit at Padgate and he, too, had been served kippers and beetroot.

R A F

2 3 7 9 5 5 8

2379558 AC1 PETER CANNON, CLERK/ GD, (January 22-March 18, 1948) has more memories than most recruits of his days at West Kirby. He was in 4 Wing, 29H Flight, and wore a yellow disc, fixed about an inch from his cap badge. 'We were some of the first National Service recruits,' he said. The Station Commander at the time was Group Captain Brian Paddon who, during the war, had escaped from a prisoner-of-war camp in Germany and made his way to Sweden where he acted as the liaison between the Swedish authorities and allied airmen who had landed in that neutral country.

Peter Cannon's boots, knife and boot brush. His kitbag, foreground, has been folded to show his service number.

His memories include going into 4 Wing NAAFI and asking Trudy, one of the assistants about boot brushes. 'We were only issued with one and I wanted another. They were still in short supply in austerity Britain, but Trudy got me one which I still use today. I still have a jar of shave cream bought in the NAAFI; I've never used it. My service table knife, stamped 1937, is still very sharp.'

Peter also has some sweet coupons which could be used in the NAAFI. They were issued by the Discip Officer - the Station Warrant Officer. 'In 1949, there was a brief period when sweets came off the ration but people went mad buying them so they were put back on ration. We also had a cigarette ration - 200 a month - packed in paper packets. The smokers were always keen to buy from non-smokers. I used to let people have mine for the price I paid for them,' he said.

'Our first meal on arrival at West Kirby was stew, served from stainless steel buckets. It was delicious.' Perhaps it was this which prompted Peter to get up early and help serve breakfast in the mess. The helpers had theirs later - with an extra sausage, of course.

'The cook in charge of making the porridge had his own way of opening the tins of Carnation milk which were to be used. He lined up the tins and then took a butcher's cleaver and pierced the lids. Effective - and quick.'

During his week of fatigues, Peter worked in the breadroom, helping slice the loaves delivered from Liverpool Co-operative Society in pale blue vans. Had he been called up two years later, Peter might have been spared the slicing. Sliced wrapped bread was introduced in this country in 1930, but was prohibited during the war as an economy measure - to save packaging, presumably. It was reintroduced in 1950. The cost of a 4-lb loaf in 1945-50, incidentally was one shilling (five new pence).

Peter did various other chores - helping to hammer Rawlplugs into the concrete floor of the gymnasium so that a wooden floor could be laid. He also worked in the armoury for a time, unpacking Lee-Enfield rifles from greasy boxes. 'In weapon training, we first used Short Lee-Enfields, fitted with a 0.22 inch tube, then Mark IV Lee-Enfields and the sten gun.

Peter Cannon

26

'On the firing range we were issued with blue commando-type cap comforters, with a steel helmet on top. I couldn't hear the sergeant clearly and when he said 'Fire', as part of the instruction, I let one go far too soon.' International events have left their mark on Peter's memory too - he recalls coming into the billet on January 30, 1948, and hearing on the radio that Mahatma Gandhi had been assassinated. Gandhi had long campaigned for Indian independence, using the method of civil disobedience. Independence was finally achieved in 1948.

One of his billet mates brought back some Perry Como records after his mid-course 48 (weekend leave) and after lights out played songs like 'Till the End of Time', 'Dance, Ballerina, Dance', and 'Dancing in the Dark'. After leaving West Kirby, Peter spent most of the rest of his service at RAF Welford, near Newbury in Berkshire; this was HQ Signals, Southern Area. He was demobbed at 101 PDC (Personnel Dispersal Centre), Kirkham, Lancashire - the place where many wartime and immediate post-war conscripts collected their demob suits. The issue of demob suits had ended when Peter was demobbed.

He went back to West Kirby in 1978 when just a few buildings remained on the camp site. 'There were bits I could still see- and I remembered the walk up the hill from West Kirby Railway Station.' He has kept in touch with eight or nine of his fellow conscripts and contacted Sgt Eric Greenwood, from Rochdale, his former sergeant DI (drill instructor) in 1997. The sergeant (probably LAC, acting sergeant) was also National Service. 'He was always immaculate but fair in manner and by nature. Sadly, he has since died.'

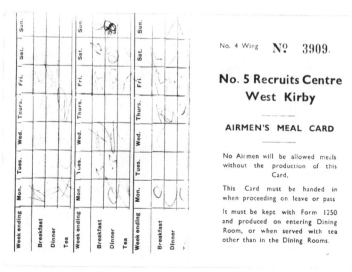

No. 4 Wing **N⁹ 3909.**

No. 5 Recruits Centre
West Kirby

AIRMEN'S MEAL CARD

No Airmen will be allowed meals without the production of this Card.

This Card must be handed in when proceeding on leave or pass

It must be kept with Form 1250 and produced on entering Dining Room, or when served with tea other than in the Dining Rooms.

Airmen's meal card issued to Peter Cannon.

27

Peter also has a note of his other former DIs. They were: Cpl M. Cullum, Streatham, London, an ex-Royal Marine with wartime service; Cpl Berwick, Luton, Beds; Cpl Hardewick, Sheffield; Cpl Stimson, Portsmouth; Cpl Campbell, Eastcote, Middlesex. They were all National Service except Cpl Cullum, who was on a regular engagement, possibly under a bounty scheme which encouraged wartime service people with experience to stay on.

Sharp Shooter

2383562 SAC JOHN TRIPP, RADAR OPERATOR, spent 23 months in the RAF, arriving at West Kirby in March 1948. He was in 4 Wing, 11J Flight. As a marksman, he was disappointed that the RAF did not recognise this by awarding him a crossed rifles badge. He had various exploits with small arms. Going round the assault course for the second time, his foot struck a lump in a hollocky meadow and he started to fall forward. His rifle, a Short Magazine Lee-Enfield, flew out of his hands and he started to go down in slow motion. 'The sergeant leapt up and down, waving his fists in fury like a little gnome, shouting 'Get up, get up.' I couldn't help laughing as I hadn't yet reached the ground.'

On the rifle range, the instructions were: 'If your rifle jams, put it down by your side; do not get up, do not wave it about and do not panic. Put it down by your side and call the sergeant.' John relates: 'One boy's rifle jammed. He panicked, leapt up still holding his rifle, spun round to look for the sergeant and passed it directly across his chest shouting 'It's jammed, it's jammed. The sergeant turned white and ordered two men to march the offender to the guardroom.'

John also used a sten gun - a simple weapon which fired 9mm ammunition on automatic or single. 'Its strong spring bounces back and forward to fire and withdraw the bullet case. This case could damage the little finger if it slid down opposite the expelling chamber so a lug was fitted to later issues.

'I fired at the target of a man. A bullet head jammed back into its shell-case. 'Pass it to me,' said my instructor. 'You are not allowed to fire a bullet impacted like that. It's dangerous, I'll do it.' He fired, removed his hand very quickly, placed it behind him and continued to face the target. After what seemed a long time, I asked: 'Are you all right?' 'Yes,' he replied. I admired him - he never made a squeak.'

John remembers the 6ft high paintings round the walls of 1 Wing NAAFI. 'They were of desert islands, pirates carousing with island women. Nothing naughty. On my next visit, to show the paintings to a friend, they had all been painted over.'

Marked Man

4061660 LAC MAURICE TAYLOR, CLERK ORGANISATION (February-May 1951) recalls being on the square, doing rifle drill under Cpl Platton. 'We were being instructed how to lay our rifles on the ground, but not being fully with it, I didn't fully understand what he had said. On the command to lay the rifle on the ground, I just put mine down. On coming to attention, I noticed the rifle was way in front of my boot - way out of line with the rest of the flight. You can imagine what sort of lecture I got from Cpl Platton. I was so embarrassed. After that, I was a marked man.'

6

'*Can Anyone Play the Organ?*'

2463646 ACI COLIN BARKER, CLERK/EQUIPMENT ACCOUNTS, was called up for National Service on March 2, 1950, and travelled from Wakefield to Padgate for kitting out, jabs and the compulsory haircut. Colin takes up the story after his arrival at West Kirby.

In the billet we were welcomed by a corporal drill instructor who told us to clean the billet, using offensive and abusive language. He would inspect the billet every hour until satisfied that it was up to standard.

'The following day we received further medical tests. Some lads were medically discharged and others had to transfer to the Army. Later, we received a welcome from the various chaplains - Church of England, Roman Catholic or Other Denominations. I went to the ODs group and was introduced to the Rev Stanley Hollis, who held the rank of squadron leader. He told us about Sunday service times on camp and said we would be most welcome.

Colin Barker, third from left, middle row. Others who signed the back of this photo were G. Barker, Todmorden (640); S. Crompton, Goole; G.C. Blount, Leeds 9; P.G. Bricheno, Bristol; Ron Cotterill, Sunderland; K.A. Atkinson; Leslie Boyle, Leeds; John Baron; A, Bradley, Hull; K. Addison, Leeds; L. Chitton, Darlington.

'I went with some friends to the service on Sunday. Before it started, Mr Hollis asked if anyone could play the organ, the previous organist having completed his training. I hesitated but as nobody else came forward, I said I would play. Afterwards, Mr Hollis said he hoped I would play every Sunday. He added: 'If anyone wants you to carry out any duties on Sundays, refer him to me.'

'We were told that a bus would be at the main gate at 6pm to take people to evening service at Westbourne Road Methodist Church, West Kirby. (Anything to get out of camp, which normally was not allowed.) A number of us went along and boarded the green double-decker bus from Crosville Motors, parked at the main gates. It quickly filled up.

'At the church, the blue-uniformed 'rookies' all trooped into the gallery. The service was led by the minister, the gowned figure of the Rev W. Garfield Lickes, a noted preacher. After service we were welcomed in the schoolroom by the youth club leader, John Bernstein, a very warm-hearted and popular figure. Among the youth group were several members of the Birkenhead Amateur Operatic Society and five singers. We had a good time together with favourite hymns, solos, monologues etc. I played the piano on a number of these occasions and at the end John conducted a short epilogue.

'The refreshments included slab cake provided by the RAF and tea and coffee provided by the church. We went back to camp by the same double-decker bus, arriving by

A Crosville bus of the type Colin Barker remembers.
This photo, courtesy of Ken Blacker, East Anglia Transport Museum, was taken in Aberystwyth.

31

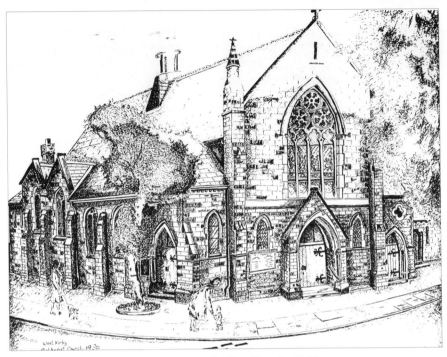

West Kirby Methodist Church, 1980.
Drawing by Richard Hempkins.

The plaque in West Kirby Methodist Church commemorating the church's link with the RAF station. It was placed in the church when the Recruit Centre closed in December 1957. The plaque was unveiled and dedicated by the Rev T. Madoc-Jones, Principal Chaplain (Presbyterian) at a service attended by members of Hoylake Urban District Council. Senior officers and men from the camp attended evening service and the CO, Group Captain C.A. Watt, read the lesson. The RAF presented the church with an inscribed pulpit bible and hymn book. Group Captain Watt presented John Bernstein (see Chapter 1) with a set of bowling woods.

(Photo: Lena Powell)

Group taken in the hall at West Kirby Methodist Church around 1950.

1 John Bernstein   2 Stella Newton   3 Joan Worsley   4 Ann Parker   5 Padre Hollis   6 Jean Sly   7 Rev. Victor Jones   8 Mrs Jones   9 Rev. Bretherton
10 Pearl Ellam   11 Ann Christian   12 Joyce Lancaster   13 Amy Ellam   14 Mr Wilfred Lord   15 Maureen Hibbert   16 Pat Houston   17 Barbara Ibbottson
18 Jean Tate   19 Jean Fraser   20 Isobel Hall   21 Muriel Baker   22 Doris Bishop   23 Ruth Ellam   24 Vera Green   25 Peter Roberts   26 John Farrell
27 Stephen Pickup   28 Eileen Wilson   29 Don Macdonald   30 John Egerton   31 Bill Christian   32 Alan Houston

10pm. Mr Hollis and his wife often invited one or two of the lads to tea at their home on Sundays and I shared in this. Mr Hollis retired to Sidmouth in Devon and I visited him whilst on holiday in Sidmouth. We reminisced about West Kirby. He has since died.' (The author remembers Mr Hollis well and also went to tea with him at least once).

The Tamer Tamed

2417590 LAC GORDON EARDLEY, CLERK GD. (December 22, 1948-March 3, 1949). 'Sgt Haugh, our drill instructor, loathed skivers - but he included in this term those who were members of the station band. We, of course, missed some of the nasty training sessions to report to the band room.

'Each morning, two of us would steal silently out of the hut at about 8am and invariably met Sgt Haugh coming from the sergeants' mess to begin his daily harassing of the lads. And every time he would treat us to a look of derision as he mouthed the word BAND..MEN (without the 's' in the middle) in his thick Irish accent. He had served in the Irish Guards, was over 6ft tall and was sometimes heard to remark: 'We tame lions here.'

'The end was approaching and the day of the passing out parade dawned. There were always two of these parades each Tuesday and the station band had to play for both. We ran straight into Sgt Haugh as we left the hut. But what a change had come over him. We couldn't believe our eyes - he actually smiled at us, came up and called us 'me lads.'

'It had been arranged that Sgt Haugh's flight would parade later in the morning following the parade of the other flight and what Sgt Haugh wanted to know was what sort of show the other lot put up. There was always an element of friendly rivalry between the NCOs of the various flights. So on this morning he became a cheery, friendly sergeant, asking us to meet him during the NAAFI break and give him a report.

'We went on our way slightly bemused and not a little worried as to just how we would report back should the other parade be faultless. As it turned out, we didn't have to worry for that other parade just went from bad to worse. For their sergeant, it was one of those mornings when nothing went right. Sgt Haugh was thus doubly delighted and almost forgot himself, nearly going so far as to shake hands with us - but then, that would never do for an ex-Irish Guardsman, would it?'

Gordon Eardley did his clerical training at Hereford, was posted to Watton in Norfolk and then to Oakington, near Cambridge. He later signed on as a regular and eventually finished as a warrant officer after 27 years service. He never forgot his National Service days and came into contact with quite a few conscripts, especially when he did a tour of duty as a typing instructor at Hereford.

Musical Moments

4063411 SAC LEN RUSSELL, MT DRIVER (MECHANIC) (HEAVY GOODS) . (March 16-May 30, 1951). Len was also a member of the station band. 'Most mornings we were detailed to report to the band room, so missing out on drill, and in the afternoons returning for whatever was taking place. On one occasion, the corporal in charge of our flight, not reckoning much to me being absent so often, with great delight told me that the next afternoon I would go through the gas chamber and over the assault course. In the band room next day I was told that in the afternoon the band would be on duty to march the Festival of Britain guard of honour out of the camp. You should have seen the corporal's face when told!

'On another occasion several of the band were returning to the band room from the NAAFI after a passing out parade so we did not have our squadron colours behind our cap badges. Unfortunately, we passed an officer without seeing him and he called us back. He asked why we didn't salute him. One quick-witted lad said that we had only arrived the night before. The officer then told us to see our corporal and be taught to salute. A near miss.'

'Any Artists Here?'

3145914 LAC NORMAN BEECH, CLERK/ORGANISATION. (March-April 1955). He writes: 'One evening our corporal came in the billet and we all stood by our beds. 'Are there any artists here?' he asked. 'Me, corporal,' I answered. Then I began worrying, in case I was to paint a fence or something. The corporal wanted a sign painted in the discipline office and asked if I had any red and blue paint at home. I hadn't, but said 'Yes.' He said I could have a 36-hour pass to collect it from home that weekend. I was over the moon: we were not allowed out of camp, let alone go home. At midday on Saturday I was off like a shot, caught the train to Liverpool, bought everything at Woolworths and then caught the train home.

'On my return the lads were envious of my luck. Unfortunately, I was to pay for my weekend at home. The board I was to paint was in the discipline office, a place of fear that no-one went in voluntarily. A corporal sat at the desk. On the wall behind him was a two-inch disc that you had to look at while being spoken to. The board hung next to a hot coke stove. I painted away, oblivious to the thump of stamping feet and the bellow of orders, reprimands and punishments being handed out.

'After finishing the red lettering, I replaced the lid on the paint tin and put it in my overall thigh pocket nearest the stove. I moved nearer the stove to do the blue lettering and heard a faint 'pop' but did not realise what it was until my thigh started to feel damp. The red paint had gone through my overalls. I raced to the washroom and tore off my overalls to find the paint was on my uniform. Luckily, I had bought a large bottle of turps and desperately cleaned my trousers. A faint trace remained but I had to get back before the corporal questioned where I was - but it was too late.

'When he saw the stain, I was reprimanded and told to go away and get rid of the stain or face the consequences. Using the last of the turps, all but the faintest traces had gone. That was the last time I volunteered for anything. The irony was that I never noticed until months later that they had given me a permanent pass; this meant I could have gone home any weekend I liked!'

7

The Man who didn't Swear

2426067 AC1 PETER HOCKING, RADAR OPERATOR.(March 17-June 10, 1949). Peter's long stay was caused by delay in his posting to Yatesbury for a radar operator's course. He was in 14Q Flight, D Squadron, 4 Wing.

He writes: 'My chief memories of West Kirby are of the RAF Regiment. Our weapons training instructors were all RAF Regiment corporals, one being Cpl Collier. We had heard of him before our first session and so were prepared for his standard opening remarks: 'I'm Cpl Collier and I'm a right b— and I swear a lot but if any of you little lads do not approve of swearing, say so now.' The lad who had drawn the

14Q Flight, 4 Wing, D Squadron, instructors and officer. Left to right, back row: Cpl R. O'Donnell, Cpl Campbell, Cpl Kemp, Cpl Stanyer, Cpl James. Front row: Sgt Ridley, (not known), Cpl Hepple. Cpl James also appears in a group photo in Chapter 10.

37

short straw immediately said that he did not. Collier's reply was: 'Right lad. I'll remember,' and for the rest of our training he did not swear once! It was probably a good PR exercise as Collier's reputation, and that of the Regiment, soared tremendously after that.

'Our flight were so bad at squarebashing that before our passing out parade we had a Regiment sergeant drafted on to the flight to bring our drill up to standard. To everyone's amazement, including our own, on pass out we won the Aspidistra Trophy as the best all-round flight. Our poor Regiment sergeant was so shattered at us winning that when we shambled back to the billets afterwards, we were brought to a halt by him shouting 'Aspidistra Flight - Whoa!'

14Q Flight, 4 Wing, D Squadron - March 17-June 10, 1949. Peter Hocking and Trevor Gay were absent from this photo. Peter has identified the following. Left to right, back row: Bill Hart, (not known), Edwin Holmes (?), (not known), (not known), Bob Evans, (not known), (not known). Middle row: extreme left, Les Hardy; extreme right, John Ferris, next to him Tich Hammond (?). Front row: (not known), Sgt Ridley, (not known), Paddy Campbell, Tex Horam. Others Peter cannot identify are: Les Goade, Brian Eccles, A. Gray, J.R. Gouge, Peter Milner, J.H. Garner, George Glossop, J. Godfrey, Mike Jones.

'Dig Your Heels In'

3512385 CPL GRAHAM PODMORE, INSTRUMENT FITTER. (February-March 1952). 'February 1952 was bitterly cold and ice had formed on the paths and roadways on the camp. Everyone was slipping and sliding along and the DI (Cpl Herd, I think) gave us his pearls of wisdom to stop this. 'Dig your —— heels in as you march and you will not slip.' To the delight of the squad, within a few seconds he had gone down.'

Cardington, February 7, 1952. Graham Podmore is second from left on front row.

'Did I Tell You I Was Regraded?'

4150921 SAC RON HODGETTS, MT DRIVER. Ron was exempt from call-up at the age of 18 because he was working in agriculture. After a family row he left home, and the farm, and eventually joined up when he was 21. But he almost didn't get in. It's a story he used to relate in the billet when everyone was cheesed off and on the moan, saying things like: 'I wouldn't join the Salvation Army after this lot.' Ron used to ask them: 'Did I ever tell you that I failed the medical and was rejected as Grade IV? I appealed and was regraded to Grade I.The boots and packs that were slung at me!'

The notice summoning Ron Hodgetts to his second medical examination.

The card which proves Ron Hodgetts was Grade I.

He was 21 when finally called up and went to West Kirby in 1954. But there were advantages in going late. 'By that time, all my mates had done or were doing their National Service. So I went to West Kirby knowing a little bit of what to expect. I took good pieces of cardboard, already measured and to cut size for stiffening large and small packs. I took spare shoe brushes and in fact spare everything else so that I could keep my kit tidy without having to use all the things which had just been issued. It helped a bit on that first evening at West Kirby when everyone was rushing around looking for bits of cardboard.'

A Visit from the SPs

2741262 CPL JOHN BAILEY, TELEPHONIST I. (December 6, 1954-February 16, 1955). John had reason to be thankful to the SP (Service Police) corporals at West Kirby. 'One evening, two SP corporals came into Hut 87 and stopped at my bed. This awesome event, in an atmosphere where DIs were gods and SP corporals even higher beings, made me very apprehensive. I could not immediately find my battledress tunic so I was told to put on my greatcoat and go with them to the main guardroom. We marched in silence. At the guard room, I was put in front of an SP sergeant, dressed in civvies. As I was answering 'Yes' and 'No' and not 'Yes, sergeant' and 'No, sergeant', one of the corporals told me to show more respect. But the sergeant said I couldn't have known his rank as he was in civvies.

'That tempered the sergeant's attitude. Instead of charging me, he lectured me on the importance of keeping my 1250 (identity card) safely in my possession. He then gave me my battledress tunic, which I had left in the ablutions, in the pocket of which was my 1250. I never misplaced it again!'

Those Little Black Flies

2392806 ACI MILROY BOUCHER, WIRELESS ASSISTANT. (June 10-August 11, 1948). On arrival, Milroy received the standard greeting, 'You'll be sorry' from recently initiated recruits. 'Then there were the DIs with their threatening voices. Because of the caps they wore, they seemed to lack eyes. Sgt Stanley, resident DI in our billet, gave us implicit instructions, in a clear Irish accent, of our expected conduct and the house rules.

'Rising at 6am, there was a shock waiting. Only cold water in the ablutions and no mirror in which to shave. On the parade ground, we endured the little black flies from the Mersey which caused agony when we stood to attention for inspection. But we survived! It made men of us and gave us fitness, discipline and respect. The memory remains - in the billet group photograph which I have framed.' After trade training at RAF Yatesbury, Milroy was posted to South Cerney, Gloucestershire, and spent the rest of his service there.

Lighter moments at South Cerney. Some of the back row are seated on a BSA 250cc motor cycle which belonged to Dave Huxtable. Left to right, back row: Jack (surname not known), Milroy Boucher (known as Bill), Paul Marchant; Dave Huxtable, Dennis Holland, Ray Tucker, Joe Walker. Front row, Dick Lines, 'Wiggy' (believed to be Derek Wigfield.)

Back to his Old Flight

3120618 CPL WILLIAM HANNA, DRILL INSTRUCTOR. (Mid-1949-late 1950). William wanted a change from penpushing so opted to become a DI. After squarebashing, he spent a short time at Hereford and then trained as a DI at Uxbridge. Asked where he wanted to go as an instructor, he chose West Kirby and found himself back with his old flight in charge of Hut B28 in D Squadron.

He met his future wife at a dance in Wallasey Village. 'I was dressed in civvies, fortunately. We would not have spoken if I had been in uniform, so she says.' They were still happily married 50 years later. Late in 1950, William was posted to Melksham and helped set up No 10 School of Recruit Training. He stayed there until demob.'I do have memories of things that happened not necessarily to me but by me. For instance, on area guard duty I used to send 'my little daft men' from D Squadron drill shed all the way to A Squadron to ask for the keys to lock the drill shed which, of course, had no doors. Then there was painting the stones white for the AOC's inspection and also tearing off a strip to someone in the NAAFI who was wearing his hat, only to discover he was a chap I went to school with. Then there was hearing a hut full of Welsh lads all singing in harmony in the evening when they were bulling up for the next day's parade. All great stuff. I had a good time and do not regret a minute of it.'

Eyes Wide Open

4126640 LAC ROY KEEN , MOTOR CYCLIST. (Mid-March to late May 1953). He still remembers the Geordie lad found lying on his back on his bed one afternoon with his eyes wide open and apparently not breathing. 'We thought he was dead but, as we were standing round him, suddenly he sat up and said that he often slept like that. What a relief!'

All Brains...

2775838 SAC BRYAN OLIVER, RADAR OPERATOR. (November-December 1955). He recalls a rifle drill session in one of the huts when it was raining. 'I was having problems with one particular movement - fixing the bayonet to the end of the rifle, I think. After a bit of frustration and fiddling, the corporal said to me in broad Cockney: 'You, airman. What did you do in Civvy Street?' Self, hesitatingly and suitably terrified: 'I... worked in a bank, C..Corporal.' Corporal (his worst suspicions confirmed): 'I thought so. All brains and no b—— commonsense!'

'I've nothing to do, Corporal'

8

5024004 SAC EDDIE HOWARD, CLERK/TYPIST. (early July-early September, 1956). Eddie reported sick because he wasn't feeling too well. The MO told him to take the rest of the day off so he went back to his billet and lay on the bed. A corporal DI came round and asked what he was doing.' I explained why I was there and said I had nothing to do. He came back a few minutes later and said: 'There are three billets here, all with rifles in them. You can clean them.' There were 32 rifles in each billet - needless to say, I couldn't clean them all. I never made that mistake again.'

On another occasion, Eddie had been to Liverpool as part of a R and I (Reliability and Initiative) test to buy something to complete his team's task. On return to West Kirby, the sentry was not at the main gate and he had to wait for admission, so he stood by the gatepost. Eventually he was let in and when 50 yards past the guard house, a voice said: 'Airman! Back here at the double.' He was asked why he had been leaning against the post and, as punishment for this supposed crime, spent the next three or four hours cleaning equipment and utensils for the guardhouse NCOs.

An Eight-week Stroll

B3516286 WARRANT OFFICER HARRY HEYWOOD, TELECOMMUNICATIONS CONTROLLER, recalls squarebashing from June 16-August 26, 1953 as an eight-week stroll. He was living at Wallasey, on the other side of the Wirral, and was a flight sergeant in 273 Squadron, Air Training Corps. West Kirby was his local RAF station and he had been there on various courses, the last in spring 1953 for training as a drill instructor in his ATC squadron.

Hut 199, 7 Flight, Trenchard Wing, passed out September 10, 1956. Eddie Howard is middle row, extreme right.

43

'When I arrived as a wet-behind-the-ears AC2, posted to C Squadron, Cpl Harding remembered me - so I feared for my future. As it transpired, it was an eight-week stroll through beautiful summer weather. I was made senior man of my billet, given various privileges and excused most drill parades. I seem to have spent most of my time painting fire buckets, cleaning the squadron offices and undertaking the duties of mail orderly.

'Being so close to home meant that my then girl friend was able to visit. My father, who was a mail van driver, timed his runs to camp so that if I had a free evening, I could get a lift to Wallasey, then catch the last bus back to the Saughall Massie crossroads, from where it was a short walk to the camp. I'd joined up with another Wallasey lad, 4129832 AC Ron Stubbs, who had a Vespa scooter. He arranged to garage it in a local farmer's barn. Whenever we had some free time, we were out of the gates and away.'

Dozing off

4178993 LAC ALAN SMITH, BARBER (January-February 1956) arrived at West Kirby from Cardington as an AC1. He had already passed his trade test as a barber at the Cardington reception unit. 'The winter of 1956 was a bad one and, stuck out on the Wirral peninsula, it was freezing but the pressure from the DIs never stopped from 6am until lights out. On one occasion, at a church service, as we were being preached to, I looked round to see nearly all the recruits were fast asleep!

'During the eight weeks, we were called to a service on camp the day the funeral of Lord Trenchard, Father of the RAF, was taking place. It was snowing heavily and freezing cold as we stood to attention with heads bowed for ages. Some of us nearly died.'

Entrance to RAF West Kirby with Gloster Meteor as 'gate guard.'

9

Short Back and Sides

4113283 LAC KEN TUFFREY, MT DRIVER (mid-October-mid December 1952) was a hairdresser in Civvy Street. He decided to take the tools of his trade back with him after a 48-hour pass. 'I thought this was a good idea. I would make a few bob (sixpence a time) and the lads would have a good haircut. In the end, I was looking after two flights out of three in the squadron.

'What I did not think about was that only a few men from G Squadron were going to the barber's shop. It did not take the barbers long to notice this and it would not be long before the guilty party (me) would turn up for his haircut. With the squadron colour behind my cap badge, I had almost given myself away. The conversation soon got round to what we did in Civvy Street; that was when I blew my cover. It was some time before I needed another haircut.'

Rabbit Fatigues

5011609 SAC PETER BROOM, CLERK EQUIPMENT ACCOUNTS reached West Kirby in May 1957 and was in Trenchard Wing. He spent a day during fatigues week in the cookhouse, gutting hundreds of rabbits. During orienteering in Delamere Forest, he earned praise for the sketches of different way points he made. 'The way points were identified by map references. You had to find them and produce evidence that you had visited them.' He also recalls the visit to the camp of Chris Barber and his Jazz Band, with singer Ottilie Patterson.

'The passing out parade coincided with the Queen's visit to Chester so, instead of a formal parade, my course carried out route lining. I was excused as I wore spectacles and I was joined by one other who didn't usually wear spectacles but found a pressing need for them in that week.' Peter's other memories include someone who had rejoined after war service and sloped around the camp wearing slippers with his uniform; a hot June afternoon on the square with people fainting, still at attention, and the DI screaming at the rest to stand still and not help them; cutting the grass with scissors - with the DI's non-favourites told to make the noises of farm animals. 'I kept my head down, or perhaps being an ex-CCF (Combined Cadet Force) cadet helped.'

Cookhouse Corn

4150932 SAC PHIL NEWMAN, TYPIST (May-June 1954) recalls getting bronzed in the 'invigorating' warm breezes sweeping across the Wirral. On a scorcher of a day, his flight were marched to the cookhouse but because they could not halt properly, at the right spot and altogether, the DI marched them up and down at least four times before they were allowed to eat. 'It seemed such a long, long time and we were so hungry.' Another cookhouse memory is of an admin orderly who told the recruits he was a sheet metal worker - in fact, he worked in the tin room, cleaning the big greasy baking tins and trays.

Narrow Squeaks

2738509 LAC ROBIN GODFREY, TELEPRINTER OPERATOR (November-December 1954) had a narrow escape from the tin room. His DI, Cpl McCracken caught him smiling on parade, marched him up and down by himself when parade finished and ordered him to the cookhouse that evening for fatigues. 'Fortunately they had finished in the tin room and I got off with just swabbing the floor in the mess hall. I also missed the experience of running around in the gas section without a gas mask on. That morning another lad and myself had to take our turn as ablution orderlies. We made the job last and when we got to the gas section, our flight were marching back, all coughing with streaming eyes.'

Winged Flight

4049841 AC1 WILLIE McFADDEN, CLERK PERSONNEL. Willie, from Northern Ireland, was not liable for conscription as the National Service Act did not apply to Ulster. He signed on for five years as a regular and was at West Kirby from July 2-September 21, 1951, in H Squadron. The CO was Group Captain Wood and his sergeant, Sgt Rogers, a sandy-haired Scot from Edinburgh. He recalls that the windows of Roosevelt mess were always open. 'Sparrows, chaffinches and an odd robin flew in and calmly strutted over the massive tables as if they owned the place.

'We used to walk down to the shore, by the Dee Estuary and watch the sun setting in the west over Ireland. As we explored, we discovered a lane; on each side was a high brick wall, with large trees towering overhead. It was our unanimous verdict that this was the loveliest courting spot we had ever seen. I think it was called Echo Lane. I wonder if it survived and how many romantic scenes those walls could recall!'

Glassed Off

2374533 AC1 DEREK NORRIS, GROUND RADAR ASSISTANT, was at West Kirby November 1947-January 1948 in 5G Flight, 1 Wing. Derek's early memory is of parading on arrival at West Kirby Railway Station. 'A small airman in front of me completely lost his balance when swinging his kitbag over his shoulder. He went flying and the kitbag hit me full in the face, cutting my nose and eyebrow and smashing my glasses. Without glasses my vision was blurred and so, with blood running down my face, we were off to camp.

'As soon as we arrived, we had the DI's kit inspection with all the yelling and shouting and one unfortunate having his mug hurled to the ground and smashed to smithereens. That night, with no glasses and a cut and bruised face, thoroughly disheartened and homesick, I hated the RAF, but it did get better. Although breaking my glasses at the time was a disaster (I had worn glasses since I was four), after about three days, my sight settled down and I never wore glasses again until I was in my 40s.' Derek's later service included a short stay at RAF North Weald during the 1949 dock strike.

All Steamed up

4079281 CPL PETER MEDCRAFT, AIR STEWARD (July-September, 1951). 'A number of my squad were detailed for area guard. We patrolled the perimeter of the camp - two hours on, two hours off. Rations were collected from the airmen's mess - tea, sugar, milk, bread and cheese. We were based in the guard hut where a pot-bellied stove burned brightly. The DI in charge sent one of the guard to fill the bucket with water. Ten minutes later he came back and asked the DI what he should do with it. 'Put it on the stove,' he replied. 'The lad then lifted the lid and poured the water into the fire. The hut filled with steam and the guard looked like the Black and White Minstrels. The rest of the night we spent cleaning up the mess.'

Kitbag Coup

2441684 AC1 DAVID BALLARD, ENGINE ASSISTANT. 2T Flight, C Squadron, August 24-October 19, 1949. 'On arrival at West Kirby Railway Station, two of us were detailed to wait with the kitbags, piled in groups according to flight numbers, and wait for the lorry which would take them to camp. After loading the lorry, we sat on the back. Seeing the steep hill out of the town, we were more than happy that we didn't have to march up it. The only bad thing was that most of the flight had dinner on arrival. We had missed ours but it was a small price to pay to miss that march.' David's flight commander was Flight Lieutenant Regelli, a Polish wartime air gunner. 'He had an artificial leg but, incredibly, marched on the square with hardly a limp.'

'Fill Those Sandbags'

2363019 LAC PHILIP LEWIS, ADMIN ORDERLY. (August-October 1947). 'The summer of 1947 was really hot and I remember going down to the beach at West Kirby and filling sandbags for use on the rifle ranges. On arrival at the camp we had seen the large glass-fronted showcase full of cups and trophies. We found what they were all about in the coming weeks. We had a PT lesson on the last period of one day and about 20 of us were put on a charge (252) for having dirty feet. We got five days jankers, but the stain on our feet was more dye from the socks than dirt, but you had no excuse in those days.'

The Humorist

4061537 CPL JOHN LYTTLE, GROUND WIRELESS MECHANIC. (March 1-May 2, 1951). 'We arrived at West Kirby on a bitterly cold day and were marched to a dirty billet. (I'm sure they messed them up for new arrivals). There we stood, cold and looking lost, when the door was kicked open by the most immaculately dressed and tough-looking corporal I have ever seen - lead weights in the trousers (to make them hang properly over the anklets), tailored battledress, the lot. Standing fists on hips, legs apart and in a voice like boots on broken glass, he barked: 'Right, you lot, my name's Jagger - pause. Then pointing to his stripes, he said 'Cpl ————' - another pause - Cpl A.B. ————. The A is for Albert and he left nothing to the imagination as to what the B stood for. He said the term applied to all his family. I couldn't stop myself laughing. He marched up to me and, with his nose about a quarter-inch from mine, said: 'What's your name, airman?' I said: 'Lyttle, Corporal.' He said: 'Well, Lyttle, when I crack a joke, it's for my own amusement, not yours, Right?' 'Right, corporal,' I said, but I noticed the slightest hint of humour in his eyes.

'A few days later, the same DI after half-an-hour's barking and shouting at our hopelessness on the square, said in a quiet voice: 'When I was a little boy, my Mummy bought me some lead toy soldiers but one day I lost my little soldiers and I cried and cried. But Mummy said: 'Never mind, Albert love, one day you'll get then back.' Then he barked: 'And, by ——, I've got them back now!' He nevertheless, turned us into the smartest flight at our passing out.'

The Sergeant's Welcome

3117863 CPL ALEC O'CONNOR, CLERK/GD. (November 19, 1948-January 22, 1949). 'I have two memories - the initial talk by Sgt Coates who, surrounded by the corporal DIs, barked cheerfully: 'This is going to be eight weeks of hell - but you'll be glad of it.' This actually turned out to be true. The second is the announcement that the Blood Transfusion Service was coming to take blood. 'They want volunteers - and that means all of you.' I still carry my donor card dated November 26, 1948.'

Alec stayed on after the end of his National Service to complete an eight-year aircrew engagement. 'I always say that the greatest single step-up in living conditions which I had was not when I was commissioned but when I went from LAC to corporal. I no longer had to eyeball the food-server to get an extra bit of bacon. In the corporals' eating place it was: 'That enough, Corp? Plenty more if you want it.' I soon realised where all the rare treats, such as unlimited butter, had been going at the Records Office where I was stationed at the time.'

Old Men of the Flight

2759004 SAC TERRY WILLIAMS, GROUND WIRELESS MECHANIC. (June-September, 1955, Hut 328, 5 Flight, Roosevelt Wing). 'I was kitted out at Cardington in the week when Colin Cowdrey, later England cricket captain, was discharged because of flat feet. I was the same size, weight, and shape as Derek Box, who came from Prescot, Lancashire, four miles from my home town of St Helens. We were issued with uniforms just one size apart - mine only just fitting, his too large. I reckon Derek, 18, got the bigger because he was thought to be still growing whereas I was 21 and assumed to be fully grown. I met Derek again, just before demob. His oversize uniform was in stark contrast to mine where to fasten the battledress top to the trousers almost exposed my knees!

The cleaning trio. Left to right, John Collis, Bristol; Terry Williams, St Helens; Leon Cox, Bolton.

'For the Reliability and Initiative test we were sent on a mapped route in the Wirral countryside. Reg, another mature recruit, was in the first position and I was back marker. Most of the lads in between us were younger and maybe looking to us older men for leadership. As we marched, several flat-backed lorries passed us. I thumbed one down and, after brief negotiation with the driver, we all boarded and kept our heads down below the shallow sides of the truck. The driver had been told where we wanted to get off, but he overshot the spot and we were dropped in sight of the checkpoint. We marched past the checkpoint but were recalled by an officer. We pleaded that we were using our initiative but were sentenced to three days cookhouse fatigues - greasy tins, tepid water and tired wire wool. Somehow, the tins were made clean enough to pass the cookhouse corporal's inspection.'

Removing the Fuzz

2451960 ACI NORMAN MARTIN, CLERK/PAY ACCOUNTS (Mid-November 1949-end January 1950). Shaving every day was a reality of service life. A rude awakening came for one recruit in Norman's billet. 'The poor lad had not yet started to shave and did not have a razor. He bought a packet of razor blades from the NAAFI and tried to remove the fuzz without the benefit of a razor - a very bloody business!' Norman was posted to Thorney Island which he found was almost a holiday camp. 'It was right next door to Hayling Island which was full of holiday camps.' (Author's Note: Norman and countless others will no doubt remember the occasional recruit who possessed a Wilkinson razor and noisily stropped (sharpened) the blade each morning before shaving.)

Just so Cold

2408264 CPL LYNDEN FLINT, CLERK/GD (October 14-December 9, 1948) recalls his first haircut on arrival. 'We were taken to the camp barber and emerged with a tiny tuft at the front with nothing much anywhere. Our forage caps felt quite big after that. The unfairness was that we had to pay one shilling (5p) for the privilege.

'I remember the cold. The wind whistled up the Dee estuary and across the camp with little to stop it. To maintain the pristine newness of the hut stoves (one at each end) there were nights before inspection when we did not light them, so that they would look shiny next morning. I particularly enjoyed the fatigues week when I was assigned to the NAAFI - the only time I was ever warm. The girls treated us with much kindness. The NAAFI and the YMCA hut were havens - though we had little money to spend from our four shillings (20p) a day. I can still identify in a flash aircraft shown in old movies from the aircraft recognition lectures we had.'

Lost for Words

2462617 LAC DAVID NALL, AIR RADIO MECHANIC (March-May 1950) recalls the experience of a fellow recruit, John Robson, a potential Oxford law student, who defied the fearsome power of the DIs. 'We were all on the square with our rifles. John ordered arms on the command 'Present arms' or some such minor mistake. Cpl Jones had his usual fit of hysterics and, squaring up to John nose to nose, screamed: 'You are a nervous wreck, Robson. What are you?' No reply from John. 'Answer me Robson. You are a nervous wreck. What are you?' John's patience was exhausted. Amid gasps of disbelief, he replied: 'I certainly will be if you shout at me in that manner.' There was a pregnant pause - Cpl Jones was struck dumb with rage. 'Insubordination, Robson. Get off the square. Move, man, move. Report to me at 5pm.' He was ordered to clean the corporal's room and polish the floor. I later overheard the corporal telling a fellow NCO that he had not known what to say to Robson as no recruit had ever answered him back before. I never heard him shout at John again.'

These two photos are from 4183055 SAC Mike Mills, MT Driver (H). He was at West Kirby from May-August 1956. The three drill instructors are left to right: Cpl Hall, Cpl Balles (in charge) and Cpl Russell. In the group photo, Mike Mills is in back row, sixth from right.

10

Travel Types and Sporting Heroes

TRAVEL and sport were always held out as two of the attractions to anyone considering joining the services. For those of us who had no choice about joining, travel was an important consideration and sport could bring its advantages. Ray Church, a colleague from my working days who did his squarebashing at Hednesford, put it like this:-

'One of the first things you had to grapple with as a National Serviceman was understanding the rail timetable - that is if you wanted to make the best use of your time off duty. At least there was in those days a fairly comprehensive rail network. Oh, the joy of getting your application form signed, your pass picked up from the orderly room and strolling (did we ever do that?) past the guard room at one minute after 12 noon on Friday with a small holdall in your hand.'

Through National Service, Ray got his first (and only) job. One of the clerks from the front counter of his local newspaper in Lowestoft had been called up and a replacement was needed. 'I applied and got the job which had to be kept open for me when I came back from my own National Service. I wonder what modern-day firms would make of that requirement?'

The Great Freeze up

3100445 LAC ALAN DUNSDON, WIRELESS OPERATOR (January-April 1947). Alan's extended stay was caused by the Great Freeze Up, which affected the whole country. 'There was no hot water for washing and shaving when there was a shortage of fuel. Sometimes we slept in all our clothes, including greatcoats, when there was no fuel for the stove - this in spite of raiding parties being sent out from most huts after dark to find wood or coal. West Kirby, with most other RAF training stations, was closed down in February because of the fuel shortage and the trainees sent home.

'I arrived home at Wells in North Norfolk on probably the last train to get into Wells for quite a while. Thereafter, the town was cut off by snow and I spent my time helping to dig out the railway cuttings on the Wells to Walsingham line until we met diggers clearing the line from the opposite direction.

'Initially we were sent home for two weeks, but this was extended on a weekly basis by BBC radio broadcasts. I think we had about five weeks leave in all. When we returned from leave, there was an intensive period of training as we had forgotten all our drill. Although not the best recruits to pass out of West Kirby, we managed - in spite of our corporal dropping his rifle on passing out parade.'

Alan recalls weekend trips to Liverpool on the train for shopping, perhaps the cinema, tea and cakes and a look at the sights. Littlewoods Store in the city was probably its only branch at that time. 'There were several good pianists on camp; they revived my interest in classical music and I joined the Music Club where record recitals were held in a very relaxed atmosphere. The NAAFI also introduced me to their tea and cakes without which I might not have survived the next two years.

'We had several cross-country runs in the snow, including one on the beach at West Kirby, perhaps to keep us moving before we froze. We had many PT sessions, perhaps for the same reason. To find the top airman in PT in our group we all had to run a mile, climb up and down the ropes in the gym, perform various exercises on equipment and throw a medicine ball about. I made it to the last four and it was then a process of elimination by climbing up and down the rope until only one was left. Not me, I am afraid.'

Alan moved to High Wycombe from West Kirby and then to a Wireless Operator, Teleprinter Operator, Direction Finder Operator course at Compton Bassett.

A Question of Geography

4183416 CPL TERRY SCOTT COLLIER, AIR MOVEMENTS (June 5-mid August 1956). 'In 1956 my home was on the Isle of Wight. After a few weeks of being taught with others to move as one on the square, home weekend leave was given - from 1600 hours on Friday until 0600 hours on Monday. Except for me. My flight sergeant for some reason thought that the Isle of Wight was in the Channel Islands, off the French coast. I was not about to enlighten him that it was only a 30-minute ferry trip from Portsmouth harbour.

'Collier,' he said, 'due to the long distance you have to travel, I've cleared it with the squadron office for you to leave camp on Thursday at 1600 hours. OK?' He added: 'I'll expect some duty-free fags for this favour.' I was to benefit from this arrangement for the remainder of my time at West Kirby. Needless to say, the flight sergeant did not receive his duty-frees.'

Travelling Time

2694119 CPL GRANVILLE JACKSON, RADAR OPERATOR (mid-July-August, 1955). If Terry Scott Collier gained his extra travelling time by mistake, Granville needed it for the 12-hour journey to Norfolk from RAF Buchan in Scotland (a distance of over 500 miles) where he went after trade training at Compton Bassett, Wiltshire. His call-up had been deferred to enable him to complete his apprenticeship as a pattern maker, engineering. He remembers the Andrews Sisters coming to sing at West Kirby camp. Like many other young men of the time, his interest in aircraft started during the war with visits to the US 8th Air Force base at Seething, Norfolk. His father was in the Royal Observer Corps at that time. Granville joined the Royal Auxiliary Air Force 2½ years before call-up. He still has his copy of the Official Secrets Act declaration, signed when he was demobbed.

Ron Runs into Trouble

3144384 SAC/CPL RON GEE, CLERK/TYPIST (September 20-November 5, 1954). Ron had been a member of the ATC (Air Training Corps) so was almost guaranteed entry into the RAF for his National Service. He had been told that listing sports as one of his pastimes would get him off all kinds of parades and duties.

'This was seized upon by the DIs and I started to train with the other runners. We had a few nice afternoons running round the local lanes, missing out on other duties. I thought 'This is cushy.' After a month, I was called into the DI's office and told that 20 of us would be going to RAF Kirkham to run in the championships. The weather was cold and wet. At Kirkham, we were told to change into running gear.

'In the changing room, some famous athletes were getting ready. I noticed that none of them wore socks with their running shoes. I thought: 'No way. I need socks with RAF-issue plimsolls - especially in view of the weather.' Off we started, down a track, up a couple of lanes and then wham, into the fields and into thick cloying mud. I realised why the experienced athletes had no socks on. I had run about two miles when my feet felt wet.

'I stopped, looked down and realised I had no plimsolls on. Panic set in. I had visions of being put on jankers for loss of Government property. As he passed me, another competitor said: 'There are some plimsolls back there.' I went back 50 yards. There they were. Everyone had run over them and pressed them further into the ground. I dug them out with my hands, finished the race and went to get changed. I then realised I had no change of socks. I changed back into uniform and left the belt on my trousers very loose so that the trousers hung over my sockless feet.

'Our bus passed through Blackpool and did not stop at the guard room. I got back to Hut 93 under cover of darkness. The socks had a good wash before the next day's inspection!' Ron's next posting was to the RAF Light Ack Ack Gunnery School at Watchet, Somerset.

Travel by Coach

For those going home on a 48-hour pass, where a warrant for rail travel was not provided, transport by private coach operators was arranged by the camp for those who wanted it. Mrs SUE MITCHELL, whose father ran Bermuda Coaches at Moreton, recalls having a lift on her father's coach at Easter to visit an uncle at Broxton in Shropshire and returning on the coach when it was bringing the airmen back. 'The coach would drive to a big hangar on the camp where all the airmen were lined up in rows. The destinations would be shouted out so that they could board the coach which would take them to their home town.' The coaches ran to Portsmouth, Plymouth and Scotland. Other firms who provided coaches were J.W. Bell of Moreton, Cox's of Wallasey and B. Lowe of Hoylake. (The author recalls travelling to Reading by coach for his mid-course 48).

Henry Edward Taylor, Sue Mitchell's father. He ran Bermuda Coaches and took airmen to Portsmouth, Plymouth and Scotland at least once a month.

Stop-start Journey

5014219 JUNIOR TECHNICIAN IAN HONEYWOOD, COPPERSMITH/SHEET METAL WORKER, (March 12-May 14, 1956) remembers his rail journey from Cardington to West Kirby. 'It was stop and start all the way. We were shunted into sidings to let the main line trains have priority. On the platform at West Kirby Railway Station, the DIs greeted us with 'Move, move, move, you 'orrible lot.' At the camp we were deposited by one of the 'holy' drill squares where a final passing-out rehearsal was taking place. We just looked on in awe, thinking we would never be able to do that.

'We were told in no uncertain terms that in six weeks we would be demonstrating this drill to our follow-up intake and, of course, we did. My call-up had been deferred until 21, to allow me to complete my apprenticeship with De Havillands as a sheet metal worker and copper-smith. After squarebashing, I was posted to Cyprus. I am glad I did National Service and, apart from one or two sad times, have many good memories, unforgettable exp-eriences and close comradeship with my fellow men.'

The ever-welcome letter from home. Note the postage rate - 2½ old pence (one penny).

Ian Honeywood, extreme left, back row. He still has the letters written to him during his two years' National Service by his family, friends and girl friends.

Knock-out Blows

3502590 SGT VERNON ROGERS, DRILL INSTRUCTOR, arrived at West Kirby as a corporal DI in June 1947 and left as a sergeant DI in July 1952. 'A few thousand recruits passed through my hands, the most famous being Percy Lewis, the British Empire flyweight boxer, and Brian Harper (son of the boxer Jack London). Brian became famous as boxer Brian London. At Padgate, Brian, identity unknown, was entered in a novices' competition and knocked out three opponents in a total of 1½ minutes. This prompted RAF Padgate to suggest that they hoped Joe Louis (world heavyweight champion) never arrived at West Kirby as he would be entered in a novices competition!

'Alex Murphy, the Great Britain Rugby League player and coach at St Helens Rugby League Club, was an officers' mess batman. I knew him well, as he passed my billet on A Squadron regularly on his way to work. I met Alex in Manchester in 2000 and we recognised each other - after almost 50 years! I captained the station Soccer first team for over three years, playing at right back.'

PTIs were the Buffer

2549534 CPL MAURICE MORRELL, PT INSTRUCTOR, was based on the big gymnasium next to the Astra Cinema and opposite the barber's shop. He describes PTIs as the buffer between recruits and the dreaded drill instructors. Among his

Extreme left, front row, is Flight Sgt Sharpe, mentioned by Maurice Morrell. Cpl Ricky James, holding the ball, was a drill instructor at West Kirby from 1948 until the station closed. He was then posted to Bridgnorth. (Photo via Norma James).

memories are the following: 'Adjacent to Pump Lane is an extensive field, used in the early 60s by Tranmere Rovers as a sports ground. Whilst at West Kirby, we set this up as football fields, using umpteen recruit squads to go backwards and forwards picking up stones, to ensure good playing surfaces.

'Flight Sgt Sharpe, a cross-country enthusiast, always ensured that his flights won the intake shield for cross-country run over Thurstaston. Some of the marks painted on posts, walls etc to mark the course, were there for over 40 years. The station had a first-rate basketball team and the matches against Hoylake YMCA were nailbiters. Both teams were among the best on Merseyside. Newton AFC benefited from the RAF presence and for many years had a nucleus of good-class footballers.

'Flight Sgt Slark, a squadron or flight instructor, retired about 1952 and was a local postman for many years. Sgt Peter Smith became a police superintendent in Liverpool. Others on the PTI staff in 1952-53 included Tony Mancini, who fought Brian Nancurvis for the British welterweight title, Cpl Taff Lloyd who became the Welsh lightweight champion, and Dai Rees who played Rugby League for Belle Vue and Wales. Cpl Ray Blick, a Birmingham PTI, built himself a canoe on camp and, as a novice, launched it on West Kirby Marine Lake. He represented Great Britain in kayaks in the 1956 and 1960 Olympics.'

Maurice also recalls Brian London as a trainee PTI and says that he won the British Heavyweight Championship and also fought Cassius Clay. A colleague has told him that the station commander suspended the station basketball team from the local league after one match with Hoylake 'which was tantamount to two teams inflicting GBH on each other'.

Happiest 18 Months

3075116 SGT JOHN INGLIS, PT INSTRUCTOR, first went to West Kirby in Spring 1946, prior to sailing for the Far East on the Mauretania in early summer. The camp was still operating as a Personnel Dispatch Centre or transit camp. He was returned to the UK in January 1947 and after disembarkation leave was posted to West Kirby, by then No 5 School of Recruit Training.

'I was seconded to 4 Wing as deputy to Sgt Joe Dowsing who was in charge of all the PT Instructors on the wing. Joe was an air gunner who had been forced to remuster in late 1945 and take a PT course. He had been trying for months to get on a master gunner's course and return to aircrew. Two weeks after my arrival, he finally got his wish and I took over as sergeant in charge of all PT on 4 Wing. I then spent one of the happiest 18 months of my life in that post, enlivened by frequent invitations to passing-out parties at the Sand Rock Hotel in New Brighton. I spent two days in the hospital

Sgt John Inglis, with heels together, demonstrating the correct balance position in front of his flight in 4 Wing hangar in early spring 1947. As a photo was being taken, eight corporals, rather than one, are walking round to encourage and correct the recruits.

Sgt John Inglis, with his fiancee, Lilian Osterman, at a passing out parade party at the Sand Rock Hotel, New Brighton. They later married.

when I broke my foot training for a PT display at Tranmere Rovers football ground. The doctor was Flight Lieutenant Ducat or Dukett. I left West Kirby on November 28, 1948, thence to RAF Kirkham for demob.'

Driver's Mate

4113369 LAC NEVILLE DAWES, MT DRIVER, as a new boy on camp, was in the driver's rest room one evening when the phone rang for the duty driver. 'He told me he had to go and pick up the CO and suggested I went with him, if only to find my way about. On the way, the driver told me the CO was interested in football and would be interested in me; not only did I play football, I was also a keen Wolves fan. At the house, the driver left me in the car. When he came out, he suggested I sit in the back with the CO so that we could discuss football. This seemed strange - to be talking to the CO as if we were old mates. When we got back to camp, I found that the 'CO' was the duty electrician, called to do a repair! It took me some time to live this down. My other memory is Cup Final Day 1953. That morning, I was waiting gloomily in the coal yard with a civilian employee, John Lloyd, feeling fed up as I would like to have seen that Cup Final. Later that day, John took pity on me and took me to his home in Hoylake to watch the match on TV. Blackpool beat Bolton 4-2 in what was known as the Matthews Final.'

11

Slow Boat from Egypt

While this book is primarily about the experiences of people at West Kirby, the author received the following stories of events from ex-West Kirby-ites which happened elsewhere which he thinks are worth sharing.

4097589 SAC ERIC EVANS, MT MECHANIC, was posted to RAF Ismailia in the Canal Zone in late 1952 and by July 1955 was due to return to UK. He takes up the story: 'Three of my pals were also time- expired. I inquired in the orderly room, but they had no information about a departure date. Then a letter arrived from my mother, giving date and time the HT Lancashire was leaving Port Said and asking why I had not told her I was coming home on it. The sailing date was the day I received her letter.

'I checked but still the orderly room had nothing to say I should be on the ship. Two hours later a teleprinter message arrived with my name on the passenger list. I had five hours to get packed. I had a lift on a lorry to Port Said, 60 miles away. On arrival at Port Said, I was asked where the other three from my section were. I had hoped to get home for my girl friend's 18th birthday, but missed it by a few days.

'When I got home, I found out how my mother knew when my ship was due to sail. Apparently, my Uncle Harry was in Lyons Corner House in Trafalgar Square in London when a stranger asked to share his table. He was Warrant Officer Dan Dewin, NCO in charge of Ismailia MT section, home on leave. My uncle told him I was there and Dan replied: 'He should

Eric Evans, standing 4th from right, outside his billet at West Kirby, circa April 1952.

be home soon' and pulled my movement order out of his pocket. He had picked it up inadvertently with his own mail, before flying home. The RAF, realising their mistake had flown my missing mates home: two of them were waiting on Liverpool dock to greet me, having been home two weeks.'

'I was eventually posted to White Waltham (the author's home village). As I was unpacking, one of the lads said 'Leave your mug on the locker because the Flight Sergeant will wake you with a hot mug of tea.' I didn't believe him, but next morning I was wakened by the Flight Sergeant asking 'Where's your b—— mug?'. He was the AOC's driver, had to be up early and brought us tea in bed every day.'

The Man who said his Prayers

2433559 AC1 RON LAWLESS, OFFICER'S BATMAN, spent the whole of his service, May 1949-May 1951, with AC1 Terry Dalby. Date of entry on their kitbags should have been 26.5.49 but the corporal in charge at Padgate, when kit was being issued, gave them the date of 5.26.49. He was demoted to LAC for this clanger.

The incident which Ron will never forget is the following. It happened at Catterick. 'A new, young face appeared in the billet. This was his first posting after trade training and his first day with us regulars of Room 4, Block D. It was latish evening. Eight or nine of us were playing cards, others were reading. The new arrival put on his pyjamas - unusual for those days when most of us just wore PT shorts in bed.

'The second thing he did was something which none of us had seen since joining the RAF. He knelt down at the side of his bed and put his hands together to say his prayers. We had one or two hard cases and characters in the billet. I thought that any minute someone would say something, or pass some lousy remark, or take the mickey. The room went very quiet until he had finished and got into bed. Then everybody carried on as normal. He did this every night and every man admired and respected him for his belief.'

'Put the Boot In'

ALEC SEED, SIGNALLER, stationed in the signals section at Bruntingthorpe airfield in Leicestershire, made an unexpected visit to West Kirby in 1944. He and a fellow airman were given a 72-hour pass and asked to act as escort for an AWOL (absent without leave) airman being held at RAF West Kirby. He recalled: 'We were issued with travel passes in order to escort our man back to Bruntingthorpe. My comrade fared well. I arrived home to find my parents had gone on holiday and I had the house to myself. Fortunately, I had brought some bacon, butter and meat from the canteen. I visited a local farmer friend and got some free-range eggs and home-made butter.

'On the Monday we collected our prisoner. He was still covered in straw. He had been in hospital and had escaped by an upstairs window and ricked his ankle. He hid in a haystack; fortunately, he was pulled out. We smartened him up and went our way. The RAF police told us: 'If he gives any trouble, use your boots.''

Dangerous Cargoes

4192904 SAC EDDIE SOAN, MT DRIVER (February-April 1957) was posted to 217 MU Bedford - a disused and derelict wartime mustard gas depot. He drove the fifth (and last) lorry each day carrying 20 tons of liquid gas to a disused railway siding where it was put on trucks for ICI, Runcorn. 'My job was to carry all the gear in case we had a leak or a breakdown, which could have included gas running down the street. None of us had a gas mask in the cab: they were all in the back of my lorry. Had there been an accident, the powers-that-be must have hoped that everyone else could hold their breath until I could get to them with gas masks etc.'

Eddie was on Christmas Island for Britain's last nuclear test - his job to take the men to work in a lorry and then unload, with a forklift, anything that arrived. 'One day a plane came in and two or more fire engines were lined up at the side and behind where I was to unload. They had foam hoses directed at the 'big box'. 'It took 40 minutes to unload and the scientists and big wigs looked greatly relieved. Thirty-seven years later I learned that the box contained plutonium.

'An hour and a half after the first H-bomb had been dropped, I was back on the airfield and a van drew up with samples from the H-cloud in lead boxes. No-one wanted to touch them so, without thinking, I picked up each one barehanded and put them on a pallet. The man in charge told my opposite number to load them on to the plane and said: 'If you can't complete in four minutes, Soan can take over. When I went for my first job after leaving the RAF, the interviewer said 'You haven't had much experience!''

The Dark Side

Most of the stories in this book recall the lighter moments of National Service, but for some people these were darkened by their experiences of squarebashing. Others have blotted out the memory from their life; several people told me they could remember nothing of those eight weeks. 3124349 SAC KEN HOPPER, Flight Mechanic (Engines), at West Kirby, November 1949-February 1950, called it the most degrading and lowest part of his life.

For 2446534 LAC PHILIP SMITH, who served from 1949-51, his memories were much more vivid. He described his basic training at West Kirby as 12 weeks of torment. Before he died in 2000, Philip sent the following account and gave the author permission to use it.

'My four course instructors consisted of an Irish sergeant, two Irish corporals and one other corporal who had had a broken romance and had signed on for life -

presumably to forget his girl friend. None of these instructors was more than 5 feet tall. I was about 6 feet 2 inches tall and weighed 16 stone. Right from the start, I felt these four NCOs seemed to take exception to me. At one stage, the corporal who had lost his loved one offered to meet me in New Brighton one evening to have a fight. We were to meet near a water container - one of those erected during the war to use in case of fires. I arrived very promptly, but he never did. Coward. I was looking forward to giving him his come-uppance.

'On another occasion, I was on drill parade when the sergeant shouted 'Present arms.' I had never heard this instruction before and therefore didn't move. The sergeant jumped from his dais and asked me what I was doing. I told him I had been in the cookhouse all day the previous day and so had not practised this movement. He retorted that I had had all night to learn and that if I did not do it correctly next time, he would wrap the rifle round my neck.

'I again failed. The sergeant, who appeared to be out of his mind, sent me back to my billet and told me to report to him at 6am next day. I did so and was handed a broom, marched to the square, brought to attention and left there. At 8am, the Station Warrant Officer asked what I was doing. I told him. He told me to return to my billet and said he would sort the sergeant out. From then on life became almost intolerable. All four instructors consistently found fault with me.

'After passing-out parade, we were told there would be a collection for our instructors and a night out at the local before leaving the camp. I was asked to contribute. I told the person collecting what I thought of the instructors and told him to take his tin away before I knocked it out of his hand. I told them I wouldn't join the booze-up with that lot (the instructors). Twice during the evening, taxis arrived trying to persuade me to join the party. Later that night two of the NCOs told me that in the morning everyone would be bussed in alphabetical order to the station and that I could go on the first bus. I told them not to bother and I would go in my turn. Having left West Kirby, I couldn't believe how sweet life could be in the RAF.'

They Got There First

12

For most of World War II, RAF West Kirby was a Personnel Dispatch Centre, or transit camp, housing airmen awaiting ship for their overseas postings. But in 1940, the station was also a reception centre for airmen of various European countries which had been invaded by the Nazis. They came here to continue the fight against Germany. (See Chapter 13 for more detail).

One of those who arrived in June 1940 was Jules Roy. He had answered the call of General de Gaulle, leader of the Free French, broadcast from London on June 18, 1940. The General had called on Frenchmen to reject the armistice between France and Germany and to fight on. Jules Roy describes his arrival at Liverpool in his book Memoires barbares (Livre de Poche). This translation has been provided by James Kirkup, author of the obituary which appeared in The Independent newspaper in June 2000, after Jules Roy's death at the age of 92.

'We disembarked at Liverpool in dense fog. Life had changed: no more sunshine - grey smoke, smells of a seaport and the tides. We were assembled on the quayside and, like good Frenchmen, continued to criticise the manias and the organisation of the British to whom we were obligated willy-nilly. Without them, whom we admired and detested ever since Mers el-Kebir, where would we have been? Moreover, as we were no longer anything, under what uniform would we have served?...

'We knew nothing of this land, few of us spoke English, so we were, mildly speaking, at a loss. At West Kirby, near Chester, not far from Liverpool, we were at first detained in a camp that was infinitely more strict than the one where, at Laghouat, our authorities had interned captured British subjects. We were subjected to a long and very searching interrogation, an almost insulting identity check. But had we not come here to support the RAF? Were we not just French citizens but accredited airmen, equal at least in every respect to the British? Definitely.

'However... We were former fighters under Petain and Darlan who did not like England. The questionings we were put through, the indifference with which we were given the once-over when all that we wanted to do was astonish by our readiness to fight - nothing seemed very pleasant to us. We could hardly believe our eyes. Iron-barred gates were shut upon us, and our officers were granted accommodation alongside the troops. We were suspected of lying, if not of spying and making false declarations until our statements were verified, compared with reports from the Intelligence Service and double-checked from fresh sources before we were inducted into the loving care of the RAF.

'Then we were free to use the mess: eggs and bacon, porridge, chips, gelatinous desserts; and we could enter the officers' lounge, with access to beaten-up armchairs and newspapers. We also had access to a bar where the beer and whisky flowed freely. In our dormitory, the nimbler ones let themselves go: pillow fights, barrack room-humour, language of the brothel. I must have been mistaken when I had thought a soldier's life was such a lofty vocation...'

Jules Roy trained in Scotland and flew with the RAF throughout the war from Elvington in West Yorkshire. He became a novelist, essayist, playwright and poet. In his novel La vallee heureuse, published in 1946, he gives an account of the nightly bombing raids, capturing the horror and the dangers faced by those who flew over The Ruhr, nicknamed by the British The Happy Valley. This was the title of the book when translated into English.

(Author's Note: Marshal Petain, mentioned above, was the distinguished World War I soldier who negotiated the armistice with the Germans in 1940 and became chief of state, setting up the Vichy Government in Unoccupied France. He was tried for treason after World War II and his death sentence was commuted to life imprisonment. The reference to Mers el-Kebir comes from an incident in July 1940 when British ships fired on part of the French fleet moored in North Africa at Oran and nearby Mers el-Kebir. Over 1000 French sailors were killed.

Purnell's History of the Second World War, Volume III, gives this information and states that at the same time French vessels at Portsmouth and Plymouth were seized. Officers and crews were sent to separate camps in the Isle of Man and near Liverpool (this must have been West Kirby - Author) where they were virtually treated as prisoners-of-war. Only a small proportion elected to stay in England and serve in the Free French naval forces. The majority were eventually returned to Casablanca in British ships and continued to serve under Darlan. Admiral Darlan commanded the French naval forces at the time of the Allied invasion of North Africa in November 1942. He gave an assurance that the French fleet would not fall into German hands and it was scuttled before the Germans could take it over. Darlan was assassinated on December 24, 1942.)

The Route to West Kirby

WHILE Jules Roy was being interrogated at West Kirby, a young man from Norwich, who had volunteered for the RAF in January 1940, was being sworn in at RAF Uxbridge. He would reach West Kirby in November 1941. When interviewed by the author in May 2000, Bernard Finch could clearly recall the detail of the 15 months between joining the RAF and receiving his overseas kit, prior to embarking for the Far East. It provides a fascinating account of service life at that time. The words that follow are largely his own. Sadly, Bernard died in June 2001, aged 85.

'In June 1940, I was ordered to report to Uxbridge for two days to undergo the ritual of attestation. This was my first acquaintance with the bell tent - 12 men slept with their feet to the central pole like the spokes of a wheel. The day after arrival, the attesting officer explained our commitment as volunteers and we took the oath of allegiance to the Sovereign, King George VI, his heirs and successors, with hand on bible. Following time-honoured practice for volunteers to the colours, we were each given the King's Shilling (5p) as an emblem in recognition of our patriotism and willingness to serve our country.

'We also undertook to fly in any type of aircraft in any part of the world. For many, this proved to be a fatal undertaking as war intensified.'

Bernard was called up on August 30, when the Battle of Britain was at its peak. He reported to RAF Cardington, Bedfordshire, and did a month's basic training at Morecambe. He was then posted to RAF Colerne, Wiltshire, as AC2 Service Police (u/t); u/t means under training. Most of his time was spent on guard duty and patrolling the perimeter. Colerne was a large airfield, just outside Bath, which was still in the early stages of construction.

'Conditions were shocking. We were accommodated in a marquee which leaked. The latrine was a pit in the open with a pole to sit on. I woke up one morning with a cracking head and found the back legs of my metal fold-up bed had sunk 6-9 inches in the soft wet ground. The airfield housed two MUs (Maintenance Units) and there were a lot of aircraft dispersed on the airfield

Cpl Bernard Finch in Colombo, April 1942. His service number was 930388.

including a Westland Lysander - a type used for landing SOE (Special Operations Executive) agents in France.

'A main gate guard duty consisted of 12 hours (1800 to 0600), with two hours on and two hours off. In the off-duty periods, I slept in a bell tent. We just piled on top of one another to keep warm. When later the camp carpenters built a hut out of two packing-cases in which Tomahawk and Mohawk aircraft had arrived from the US under the Lease-Lend scheme, we still huddled in one corner!

'All this time I was waiting to attend a police course at No 1 RAF Depot, Uxbridge - regarded as the Aldershot of the RAF. This came up in February 1941 and I spent hours on the square under the watchful eye of a retired Coldstream Guards sergeant drill instructor. Discipline was very strict. Because a number of airmen had been killed when a bomb fell on the Hammersmith Palais de Danse, Hammersmith was out of bounds to the trainees. One man who broke the ban was given a week's jankers (confined to barracks) and had to whitewash the coal in the guardroom in addition to other punishing chores.

'Uxbridge was a prewar RAF station and the accommodation in barrack blocks was good; the food was awful. (It was here that Lawrence of Arabia did his initial training after enlisting as an aircraftman after World War I). At the end of the course, I passed out as LAC (Leading Aircraftman) with the rank of acting corporal. I took the stripes home and my mother sewed them on.

'My next posting was to RAF Bircham Newton in Norfolk - a Coastal Command airfield equipped with Blenheim bombers used to raid German shipping off the Dutch coast. German bombers returning from night raids on the Midlands were intercepted over the North Sea by British fighters and many aircraft were brought down just off the English coast.'

Bernard and his colleagues could be detailed for the unpleasant task of recovering bodies washed up on the shore at Brancaster. Some had been in the water for up to a fortnight. The German airmen were buried in Great Bircham churchyard with a military funeral service, their coffins draped with a swastika flag on the way to the burial. Their bodies remain at Great Bircham, although many of their colleagues shot down elsewhere were subsequently transferred to a German cemetery at Cannock in Staffordshire.

Just before he moved to West Kirby, a Blenheim taking off from Bircham Newton stalled when it was only 20-30 feet above the ground. When it hit the ground, one engine blew up and a 500-lb bomb it was carrying blew up. Bernard and a corporal, Bob Major, were running towards the aircraft but, fortunately for them, the blast all went in the opposite direction. It was sufficient to blow the other engine a quarter of a mile. The wireless operator/air gunner, Sgt Len Glasscock, survived the crash and, years later, Bernard contacted him at Stansted.

Bernard takes up the story: 'On arival at West Kirby, we were allocated to wooden huts bordering one of the five squares. One of the huts was flying a red flag as there had been an outbreak of meningitis within. This hut was out of bounds. As Hitler had invaded Russia by this time, the immediate threat of an invasion of Britain had gone and so reinforcements could be sent to the Middle and Far East.

'We slept in free-standing, rickety wooden double-decker bunks, roughly put together and loose at the joints. Instead of springs, the base was wire-netting - and it sagged. We were hauled out at 6.30am every morning for PT. The parade ground was shrouded in fog and there were small frozen puddles on the surface. The new arrivals were formed into drafts - that is, groups who would be travelling together to the same overseas destination. Each morning, the drafts formed up on the square for colour hoisting (the raising of the RAF standard) and were given orders for the day. There was a roll-call every morning - to check no-one had deserted.

'The day's programme could include lectures in the camp cinema, particularly on the dangers of VD (venereal disease). The MO urged recruits not to go with native women, because of the risk, and the chaplains stressed the moral angle of intercourse outside marriage. At one point, tropical kit was issued. This included a topee (a wide-brimmed, high-domed sun helmet with a flap at the back to protect the neck). This type was first used in the Boer War and was called the Wolsey helmet.

'They were heavy and not popular with the lads who bought their own much lighter planter's type helmet when they reached the Far East - price one rupee. The tropical kit issued at West Kirby included two pairs of shoes, two khaki drill bush shirts, two pairs of khaki drill shorts, two pairs of stockings and two pairs of cellular trunks. The vests were thick flannel. We were told they would absorb the sweat. My guess is they had a surplus of these and no cotton vests. We didn't need either when we reached a hot country.

'After a short time, they would take the tropical kit in and issue us with Polar kit. We were told we might go to Iceland or somewhere near the Arctic Circle. But we had the tropical kit back again before we finally embarked. Some entertainment was provided on the camp, including a concert by ENSA artistes. I remember visiting the Ranelagh Forces Club near Liverpool Central Station. I saw Henry Hall and his orchestra at the Liverpool Empire Variety Theatre. His singer was the young Betty Driver who, in the 1990s, was appearing as the barmaid in The Rovers Return in TV's Coronation Street. I also remember a ventriloquist, Arthur Prince. Both he and his dummy, Jim, were dressed in naval uniform. Sir Harry Lauder also appeared with his repertoire of Scottish stories and songs. The audiences were noisy and constantly made disparaging remarks about the performers.'

Bernard and a pal, LAC Norman Jones, wireless operator, were friendly with two nurses, one of whom was Louise Williamson, from Smithdown Road Hospital. 'We once took them to tea at the Adelphi Hotel. This was out of bounds to other ranks (those who were not officers) but nobody said anything. I also attended concerts at Liverpool Philharmonic Hall - admission to Forces two shillings and sixpence (12½p). Years later, I saw a TV documentary of one of these concerts with Sir Malcolm Sargent conducting the Liverpool Philharmonic Symphony Orchestra and Dame Myra Hess playing Grieg's Piano Concerto. I clearly recognised myself sitting behind the orchestra in the seats allocated to the Forces.

'To ensure each draft contained the ranks and trades that were wanted at particular overseas locations, the drafts would be called together in the evening. On one occasion, they asked for two RAF police. I saw a chap I had been at school with in Norwich step forward. I started to go forward to join him but someone else got there first. The draft went to Canada - but you didn't know the destination when you stepped forward. I later wished I had been quicker off the mark.

'One Thursday evening, we were told we were going on embarkation leave next day until Monday 23.59 hours. It took nearly all day to get home to Norwich by train. I came cross-country via Crewe and Peterborough and finally on the old M and GN (Midland and Great Northern line) via Melton Constable.

'I went back Sunday night. We were due to sail from Greenock on the Clyde because Liverpool docks had been so badly damaged in the air raids in November. All carriages were locked on the train which took us right into the dockyard of King George V Dock. I jumped off and went through a large shed teeming with MPs (Military Police). You went in one end and out the other, then up the gangway on to the ship. The last thing they took from us were our identity cards - 1250 in RAF parlance. Later we were issued with pay books. The book contained a will form. If completed, this was valid and did not need witnesses. There was also space to enter details of VD infection. This was regarded as a self-inflicted wound and pay was stopped accordingly.

'We had been issued with two kitbags: the one with two blue rings painted on it was 'not wanted on voyage.' This was known as the deep sea bag and was stored in the hold. The other, with one ring on it, we kept with us. We were given cabins and shown where to find them. Deserters who had been arrested were brought on board in handcuffs. MPs remained on gangway guard all night until the ship sailed at daybreak.

'Our ship was the Athlone Castle, a 25,000-ton liner of the Union Castle Line, pressed into service like many others as a troopship. We were told it had been selected to carry mail to South Africa prewar as it could reach the Cape of Good Hope in 13 days. In our wartime convoy, it took a month to reach Durban.

'Another liner was under construction on the Clyde and, when there no air raids, work went on all night by floodlights. Before leaving West Kirby, I had asked the sergeant where we were going. He wouldn't tell us but said: 'You will still be on the sea in six weeks.' We were - our draft destination was Singapore.

'We boarded the ship on December 7. That night, they announced that the Japanese had bombed Pearl Harbour; this brought the USA into the war. We sailed next day and became part of a convoy of 200 ships with 50 or 60 escort vessels. Some were old US destroyers supplied under Lease-Lend. The convoy included all sorts of vessels, including oil tankers returning empty to USA, plus a battleship and an aircraft carrier. My last sight of land was County Antrim, Northern Ireland, and the Mountains of Morne.

'Some of the ships carried Walrus amphibious aircraft. We were circled once by a German Condor reconnaissance plane. The convoy then changed course and we went north to Iceland to avoid U-boat packs. Ten days later, on a southerly course, we were in sunshine. We passed the Azores and made our first stop at Freetown, Sierra

The RMMV Athlone Castle in which Bernard Finch sailed to South Africa in 1941.

72

Leone. We anchored a quarter-mile offshore - out of range of the mosquitoes. We were not allowed ashore.

'The next stop was Capetown. I saw Table Mountain with mist on top - a wonderful sight at 8 am. We then sailed to Durban where the harbour was crowded with ships including the New Mauretania.' Bernard's unit was thought to include a radar unit. It included men in various trades who had come to West Kirby from RAF stations throughout Britain. When they reached Singapore on February 5, 1942, on the City of Canterbury, the Japanese were already in the north of the island, preparing a full-scale offensive. At that stage, the Japanese knew little about radar.

Bernard sailed on to Java on February 7, escaping capture when the island was invaded by the Japanese. He was subsequently evacuated from Java in a destroyer, HMS Kedah, which broke down in the middle of the Indian Ocean and drifted for four days before being towed by a Royal Navy cruiser to Ceylon (now Sri Lanka). Bernard stayed there until December 1944. But that is another story! From leaving West Kirby to seeing his parents again in Norwich in January 1945, three years and one month had elapsed.

(Author's Note: To emphasise the servicemen's contempt for the Wolsey helmet, Bernard added this derisory sequel: 'The voyage from Colombo, Ceylon, to England in December 1944, when my tour of overseas service ended, was routed by troopship through the Suez Canal. The decks were crowded with airmen having a last look at the canal as we sailed out of Port Said. Suddenly, a loud cheer went up as a long train of khaki shapes leisurely drifted astern of the ship and headed down the canal on a southerly course. Yes - you've guessed it. It was the final demonstration of disapproval as scores of Wolseys were discarded and sent on their way back to the Red Sea. I understand that this continued a long tradition observed by all troopships bearing time-expired airmen 'bound for Old Blighty's shores.'')

Prunes and Custard

WAAFs were part of the permanent staff at West Kirby during the war. Kathleen Hazlewood (nee Doran), who was from Liverpool, joined the WAAF (Women's Auxiliary Air Force) in August 1942 and, after initial training at Innsworth, Gloucester, was posted to West Kirby for the duration of the war. She became good friends with Mary Bradshaw, also from Liverpool, and they spent most of their free time together. Mary later became her sister-in-law. Both were waitresses in the Overseas Officers' Mess. 'We were kept busy with the many officers who were waiting to be served their meals at different times - sometimes in the early hours of the morning, or late at night. We had some laughable incidents at times - especially on Christmas Day, when the officers waited on us at dinner time.

73

'One day at lunch, we had 100 officers in the mess. Prunes and custard were being served as a sweet and some custard had been spilt on the floor. Unfortunately a girl named Stella slipped on it. She had about four sweets in her hands and, as she fell, she was covered in prunes and custard. One of the officers said to her: 'You have given us something to laugh about when we are on the ship going overseas.' This really added insult to injury. Stella retorted: 'None of you has asked me if I have hurt myself.' Thankfully, she hadn't.

Kathleen considers the WAAFs were well catered for on the camp - with dances, the cinema and the YMCA to go to. Kathleen married Arthur Hazlewood, her boy friend before she joined the WAAF, in June 1945. The chef on No 4 Wing made a three-tier cake for their wedding. 'He put it by the open window in the store room and as the kitchen was on the edge of the parade ground, some bright spark walked off one evening with the top tier. We were working late that night and Jock, the chef, thought one of us was trying to be funny and he was really angry. We never found out who the culprit was.'

Wartime WAAFs at West Kirby.
Left to right:
Joan Taylor, Betty Richards, Mary Bradshaw, Joan Kilvington, Kathleen Doran.

History of the RAF Station 13

INFORMATION from files at the Public Record Office, plus reminiscences of service people stationed at the camp and civilians associated with it, are contained in this chapter. They provide a fascinating history of the camp and its impact on the surrounding area.

THE PRO files record that the advance party to open up West Kirby as No 5 Recruits Centre arrived on April 25, 1940. The first recruits arrived for training, based on a three-weeks syllabus, on May 16, 1940.

A member of that advance party was 981865 AC2 FRED NEGUS. He had been called up and reported to Padgate on March 12, 1940. He did his squarebashing at Morecambe where quite a few of the Blackpool footballers were drill sergeants. At the end of squarebashing, the sergeant major read out the list of postings; Fred and 19 others were to go as the advance party to a new RAF station at Saughall Massie. Fred, who had been rambling in the Wirral prewar, knew that Saughall Massie was not far from West Kirby. As no accommodation was available at the new camp, the advance party stayed for a week in married quarters at RAF Sealand, near Chester.

They then set out in a canvas-topped three-ton lorry and arrived at Saughall, near Queensferry - just a few miles away. On inquiry, they found there was no RAF station; their destination was RAF Saughall Massie and they arrived at what, to avoid confusion, afterwards became known as RAF West Kirby. (Author's Note: a wartime plan of the camp bears the name RAF West Kirby (Saughall Massie)).

Fred takes up the story: 'We were confronted with a large building site of 150-160 acres. There was just one hut ready for occupation. We were classed as ACH/GDs (Aircraft Hands, General Duties). Just two people had arrived ahead of us - a warrant officer and a sergeant. The warrant officer told us that we were the nucleus of the permanent staff and that there was no reason why we should not remain there for the rest of the war. This suited me down to the ground as I came from Liverpool - just 12 miles away.

'There was no fence round the camp. The builders were Wimpeys, a large national building contractor. We did all manner of jobs. As the huts were completed, our main job was to go to West Kirby Goods Station and bring back all the stuff that was needed, such as beds, mattresses, tables etc, for stocking the huts.

'The first batch of recruits arrived on May 16. From May 31 to June 24, I and several others were assigned to be SPs (Service Policemen). The sergeant in charge, Sgt Meadows, was a service policeman by trade and he needed us to help him run the show until he got some proper policemen posted to him. We wore armbands with SP on them and most of the time we were checking that the recruits were correctly dressed before they went out of the camp. Little did they realise we had only been in the RAF a few months - and they were terrified of us.'

The PRO files record that during 1940 the station was used as an assembly point for Polish Air Force personnel evacuated to England. Fred has a note in his diary that they arrived on June 25 and 26 and left on July 1 and 2. He believes most were aircrew who joined RAF squadrons. 'Although they used the HQ mess, we did not have much to do with them. On July 5, myself and others were put on gunpost duty and that is where I stayed until I eventually left West Kirby and was posted overseas.'

'On December 13, our gang were promoted to AC1 and we celebrated on December 20 with a meal in New Brighton. That was the night when New Brighton had its worst air raid of the war and we had to walk all the way back to camp. On December 22, there was a bomb scare with an unexploded bomb on the camp but, to my knowledge, the camp was not hit again throughout the rest of the war. There were many big raids on Liverpool which we could see when we were on night duty in the gunpits. There were times when the sky was completely red with all the flames over the city. We used to sneak off home as often as we could because, naturally, we were worried about our people at home. I used to take some of the Scottish lads home with me occasionally and my mother would put on a bit of a feed for them as a change from the camp food.

'On February 22, 1941, we were remustered to be aircraft hand/ground gunners and got our badges which were a bit unusual at that time. It was a round piece of cloth, worn on the arm, with a wreath round the outside and the letters GG in the middle. This was quite different from the air gunner's badge, with a single wing and the letters AG, worn on the breast of the tunic. People used to stop us in the street and ask what our badges were. We had to reinforce all the gunpits and went to Hoylake shore, filling up sandbags. Flying Officer Purdy was in charge of the gunners. There were nine gunpits in all, equipped with Lewis guns. They were about eight feet in diameter, made of brick and concrete, about five feet high, with a small dug-out about six feet long and four or five feet high. The whole thing was surrounded by earth and sandbags. A lot of my time was spent in the gunpit near the outdoor rifle range. When the recruits were firing, we had to wear tin hats. Although we were behind the direction in which they were firing, many times their bullets missed the sand and hit the surrounding wall, bouncing back about 50 yards and landing in our gunpit. The bullets were extremely sharp pieces of metal; we used to collect them and keep them in matchboxes.

'Most of the recruits had never fired a rifle before and were terrified of the recoil and the bang. Some of them did not hold the thing firmly and this was what caused the trouble. Opposite the main gate was a rifle range for 0.22 shooting which only the officers used. It was open to us because we were gunners and one of our chaps, Bob Simpson, was a gamekeeper from Crieff in Scotland. With a 0.22 rifle on a 25-yard range he could hit an old penny right in the middle every time.'

Official records show that West Kirby received instructions on February 7, 1941, to prepare to close No 5 Recruits Centre in readiness to open No 1 Personnel Dispatch Centre (PDC). The advance party for that unit arrived on February 19. Most recruits had been dispersed to other centres by March 1 and the training of the remainder continued until June. In the meantime No 1 PDC had formed and the first overseas drafts in that unit started assembling on March 3.

This ties in exactly with Fred's diary: 'On March 3, the PDC people started to arrive. The camp used to fill up and then eventually the whole lot would move out one night to get the ships in the Mersey and join big convoys. While the PDC people were there, there were so many people on site that they extended the camp by putting tents into fields down towards Saughall Massie. A new gunpit was made from sandbags, halfway towards Saughall Massie. (Author's Note: Tented accommodation for 2000 personnel was provided from April-October 1941. In March 1941, the camp had been converted to the dual function of recruit training centre and PDC. It ceased to act as a recruit training centre in June 1941).

'The camp had been fenced months before. The bounds of the camp (the area you could go into without needing a pass) were Moreton, Meols, Hoylake, West Kirby, Frankby, Greasby, Upton, and back to Moreton. Needless to say, the Liverpool lads used to find ways and means of getting home without a pass. We knew all the ropes for getting across the river and dodging the SPs. I used to cycle home through the Mersey Tunnel and I rode right through it once without seeing a soul. This was while I was getting back during an air raid. During the bad raids, you could see the sky glowing red over Liverpool. I had some amazing adventures on those trips, all of them without a pass, and I never got caught. 'Many a night was spent on duty in the freezing cold, and you had to keep your wits about you in case the orderly officer came round. You had to keep your head above the dug-out in case he caught you scrounging! There wasn't much chance of any parachutists coming down - that's what we were supposed to be there for. And there wasn't much chance of any low-flying aircraft either.

'I can't remember many names but a few that occur to me are Ernie Arrowsmith from Blackpool, Wally Washbourne from Liverpool, Billy Thorburn from Aberdeen, Jack Charlton, from the London area and Bert Lofthouse, the elder brother of Nat

Lofthouse, the footballer who played for England and for Bolton. A couple of our lads married NAAFI girls.

'From April 4-26, I was posted to the Isle of Man for a gunnery course - one week in Douglas and two weeks in Castletown. We did all kinds of work on Lewis guns, Vickers and ground-to-air photo-guns and so on. June 1 - promoted to LAC. On August 26, the Squadronaires were at the camp. I had seen them at Morecambe. (Author's Note: Jimmy Miller, who was the leader of the Squadronaires, died in April 2001, at the time Fred was preparing this information. His obituary in The Times states that the band was composed of British dance band musicians who had been encouraged at the beginning of the war by Squadron Leader O'Donnell at RAF Uxbridge to join up and form a service orchestra to entertain the troops.)

'In the second half of 1941 we had two or three ENSA shows in the camp but nobody famous was in them. We went to sports meetings at The Leas School (see Appendix III) in Hoylake. We were in competition with the school and local Army units. I ran for the station twice. In early 1942 I was on parade for a funeral in Heswall for an aircrew member who had been killed. We acted as bearers.

'The CO at West Kirby was Group Captain Jones, if I remember correctly. On one occasion we were told his son had been killed flying and he had a piper going round HQ building all day playing laments in honour of his son. On March 4, I was posted to Blackpool ready to go abroad. On March 20, we went to Greenock and from there to India. We disembarked at Bombay on May 22 and immediately went to Calcutta and the forward area at the time which was in what is now Bangladesh but was then Bengal. I spent most of my time on the border between India and Burma and eventually left Bombay on December 20, 1945, arriving back in Blighty on January 14, 1946. I was discharged on March 11 - six years to the day from when I joined up.'

Wartime plans of the camp show that there were four parade grounds - one for each wing. Fred believes that the fifth parade ground, which two other contributors to this book have mentioned, may have been for HQ staff. (It is marked as 'Station Parade Ground' on the administrative order for the final passing out parade, held on December 20, 1957). Since getting his first car in the 1950s, Fred has been across to the Wirral many times and passed the old camp hundreds of times.

Barrack Damages

ERIC WILSON, who left school in 1938 and started work for a local builder, remembers how the smaller firms lost men to the camp site as work got under way to build the new RAF station. During the war, Eric was sent to work in London and Kent, repairing war-damaged properties. After the war, he returned to Great Meols and did maintenance and repair work at the camp from June-October 1957. Many of the huts needed new threshold steps at the entrance. 'I suppose that with all the men going in and out in their heavy boots, the thresholds got worn away in next to no time. The outsides of the huts needed new boards pieces or small sections.

'Like many of the workmen and officials on the camp, I think they had been kicked in at night by lads who were drunk and couldn't be seen. Inside, big holes had been kicked in the plasterboard walls. Sometimes a lock needed replacing on a door. Everything we had to repair or attend to was typed on a jobsheet - even putting a grub screw through the handle of a door lock. The same applied to plumbers working on wash basins and electricians dealing with light switches. I only worked at the RAF hospital on two occasions. I suppose people in there were better behaved so didn't smash things.' Eric also recalled the small wooden hut at the top of the bridge at Meols Railway Station which was the taxi office and how the lads scrambled to get into the taxi back to camp.

Fun Cut Short

ALBERT HALL started work at the camp in 1942. He had hoped to become an electrician but most of the large electrical firms told him they could take him as an apprentice but could not guarantee employment when their other apprentices came back after the war. Instead, he became a plumber, following the trade of his uncle who worked in the Cammell Laird Shipyard. As a child, Albert lived opposite the Black Horse Hotel on Blackhorse Hill. 'In winter, we had great fun taking our sledges to the top of the hill; with a good push, we would finish up part way along Camp Road. Once the camp was built, the council started to grit the road, so that was the end of that. I recall the Polish airmen who used to march from West Kirby Railway Station to the camp. As children we sometimes marched along with them, collecting their autographs. It was very noisy when the rifle range was in use; we could hear the firing from our house.'

NAAFI Memories

BARBARA SMITH was employed by NAAFI at the camp from 1942-47 as a clerk in the office attached to the grocery shop and warehouse store. Barbara visited the four wings twice a week to collect the money for banking from each canteen. She has many happy memories of meeting people from all over the country. 'As it was a transit camp, people used to come and go so quickly. I met my husband there at a dance in the YMCA and we were married in 1948 at St Bridget's Church, West Kirby, by the RAF chaplain, the Rev Patrick J. Macken.' (Author's Note: In addition to the YMCA canteen on camp, there was also a WVS canteen next door to Westbourne Road Methodist Church in West Kirby in part of a house now incorporated into the church, and also a YMCA canteen in the premises which, in 2000, were occupied by the Abbey National).

Hoylake District N.A.A.F.I. R.A.F. Station No.5 R.T.C. West Kirby

Barbara Smith, extreme right (in white blouse) third row, has supplied this photo of staff from the Wing canteens taken in 1946. Also in the picture are: back row, extreme left, Bob Smith, storeman; next to him the late Nancy Rainford, shop assistant. Third row, extreme left, the late Mavis White, shop assistant; next to her, Winifred Jelly, office. Second row (all seated) fourth from left, Mr Kinvig, office and store manager; seventh from left, Kit Wright, canteen manageress; third after Kit Wright, Olive Stewart. Olive was in the ATS and visiting West Kirby en route to somewhere else.

Family Link-up

SOME of the airmen at the camp were offered hospitality by families in the area. Wilf Mino, from Canada, knew he had distant relatives in the Liverpool area. He made contact with them and spent his leaves with the Thomas family, then living at Anfield, Liverpool. Mrs Edith Thomas recalls that her then boy friend, Ronald Thomas, used to take Wilf out on his tandem to explore the area. He was later posted to India. On his return to England, he again visited the Thomas family and kept in touch after going back to Canada. Mrs Thomas and her husband visited Wilf and his family many times. Wilf, who ran a successful lumber company at Georgetown, Ontario, died in 1981.

Post-War Pioneers

When West Kirby became a recruit training centre again, the first batch of 469 recruits arrived on September 10, 1946, and went into E Squadron, 3 Wing. Fifty-one corporal DIs had arrived from Cardington the previous day. Training started two

1947 aerial view of RAF West Kirby.
(Photo via Trevor Oldroyd)

days later. To provide accommodation for the total number of recruits who would be under training in the future, the buildings of the overseas officers' and sergeants' messes were closed awaiting approval for conversion work. A further 469 recruits arrived on September 11; 457 on September 17; 460 on September 24 and 471 on September 25.

Problems arose over catering. At the end of September instead of the 101 cooks allowed for in the establishment, only 44 had arrived. An urgent letter was sent to Group HQ, requesting immediate action.

Among the recruits in that first intake on September 10 were Harry Catling and Roy Furby. They did not meet then, but made contact in 2001 through the Channel 4 Ceefax link-up, Service Pals.

3088047 AC2 HARRY CATLING had arrived at Padgate a week earlier, hoping to become an air traffic controller. He recalls: 'The RAF was knee-deep in redundant traffic control bods so, on the advice of one of the interview panel, I opted for radar/ wireless mechanic and became an AC2 G/D U/T RWM - the longest title I'd ever had. At Padgate, where we were kitted out, it seemed to be raining constantly and we stood in vast queues in immense hangars, clutching mug and irons (knife, fork and spoon) and cheering loudly when someone dropped his mug.

'At West Kirby Railway Station, clad in greatcoats and 'change of station order', beneath the blazing autumn sun, we were met by screaming corporals, clutching clipboards. They formed us into constantly changing ranks and squads. The squads marched off but the last two files of our squad were lopped off and a large sergeant told us that we were to 'load the kitbags and ensure their safe arrival.' We loaded them into a lorry and were driven to the camp. After unloading, we were allowed to sit and smoke until the unlucky marchers arrived. Still in their greatcoats, they were soaked in sweat and scarlet in the face. As they marched on to the parade ground, they dropped like flies. It was probably the most strenuous exercise most of them had ever had.

'We were allocated to our huts - alphabetically, I think, because in my hut we were all Cs. One of my hut mates was Arthur, a former monk, who had lost his faith and signed on as a regular. We swopped underwear. I had been issued with hairy, flannelette long johns and vests which went to the bottom of my kitbag while I continued to wear my civvy garb. His were Aertex type, something he had never worn before and regarded with horror. We each thought we had the best of the deal.

West Kirby
Railway Station in 2000.
(Photo Dr James D. Jones)

West Kirby
Railway Station interior.
(Photo Dr James D. Jones)

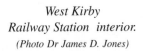

82

'Bob Carson, a Scot, and an amazing trumpet player, became my best mate at West Kirby. We were once put on a charge for slipping a clip of dummy rounds in another recruit's rifle. During arms drill, on the command 'Ease springs' he sprayed our Cpl Moorhouse with five dummy rounds. We each got seven days jankers. Most of our NCOs were not proper drill instructors but fitters and other trades, newly back from the Far East and more interested in getting demobbed than giving us a hard time. We spent more time building a rifle range than squarebashing. This pleased us greatly as the weather was marvellous. One NCO I remember was Flight Sgt Knight - he used to wrestle in Liverpool, Manchester etc, as The Black Knight.' Harry Catling was a civilian employee of the Ministry of Defence (Air) after demob and lived in West Kirby in 1970 in Douglas Road, just off Black Horse Hill, the former RAF officers' married quarters.

Balloons over Birkenhead

JIM SIMPSON was four when World War II started in September 1939. He knew one of the families, the Days of Larton, some of whose land was compulsorily purchased to form part of the site of the RAF station.

His uncle, Frank Shackleton (known as Barney) was employed on camp construction etc, as a joiner early in the war. He returned to that position after service in the Army and subsequently became clerk of works in charge of maintenance and repairs. He was employed on the camp until 1957.

Jim moved away to Bristol for a while where his father was working in an aircraft factory for the Bristol Aeroplane Company, but from 1944 he lived in or near West Kirby.

'From the time I first saw barrage balloons in the sky over Birkenhead, the war was a part of the background. From my angle, it was almost as though it had always been there. The six years up to August 1945, when Japan surrendered and the war was finally over, was a huge span of life to a child.

'Airmen of many different nationalities passed through the camp and could be seen in West Kirby any day of the week. The uniforms were of almost every shade of blue. Those from the then countries of the British

West Kirby, June 1953.
Left to right, AC2 Jim Simpson; AC2
Pete Davies; (not known).

83

Empire, like Canada, Australia, New Zealand and Rhodesia, wore a shoulder flash with the name of their country on it.The Australians stood out because of their dark blue uniforms. There were Poles, Czechs and others and this was the first time I had heard people speaking in a foreign language. Later, there were American servicemen, too. In fact, I used to keep a weekly score of the different nationalities I had seen.'

One other feature of wartime life in and around West Kirby, recalled by Keith Fullarton, a school pal of Jim's, was the large number of RAF vehicles. There was no petrol ration for private motorists so civilian vehicles on the road were only those classed as essential users - and there were not many of them.

As an ATC (Air Training Corps) cadet in No 2184 Heswall Squadron, Jim attended a ground combat training course at RAF West Kirby and also did rifle shooting on the range. On call-up in 1953, he was posted to West Kirby for squarebashing. A parade was planned on the camp for the Coronation of Queen Elizabeth II on June 2 of that year. 'That morning, an announcement was made over the Tannoy that Mount Everest had been climbed by Sir Edmund Hillary and Sherpa Tensing in a British expedition led by Colonel John Hunt. To ensure that those on the national parades had the best webbing to wear and the best rifles, bayonets etc, everyone's webbing was called in and the best was chosen. These items were used by RAF personnel on Coronation route lining and parade duty in London and for the RAF Coronation Review at Odiham, Hampshire. Those who took part in the Coronation events were issued with barathea uniforms. This led to the gradual replacement of serge best blue with barathea and the issue of a raincoat. NCOs down to the rank of corporal were the first to benefit.

'The rifles we were left with were very rough and it was some time before we received a full set of webbing again. There was a similar quality check on bayonets, with the result that we received just two hours of bayonet drill at the end of the course. 'After the Coronation Day parade, the recruits were given the rest of the day off. Jim walked home and watched the Coronation ceremony from Westminster Abbey on an aunt's TV. Later in his service, Jim returned to RAF West Kirby, this time as a patient in the hospital (see Chapter 14).

Looking back on the impact that the camp made on the district, Jim reflected: 'Anyone who lived on the camp side of West Kirby and Grange Hills will recall that the camp generated a lot of noise. Depending on wind direction, shouted orders and the responses of the trainees could be heard over quite a wide area.' Jim also commented on the suggestion that the RAF station might once have been called RAF Larkhill, although there is no evidence for that in the PRO files. He thought it could only have happened if there had been some kind of anti-espionage ploy to dissuade the enemy from pinpointing targets.

A Patchwork of Badges

JOHN GITTINS has a record of his three years delivering newspapers to the camp. It is a patchwork of the badges he collected from airmen of various countries who were stationed there. To these he has added other wartime badges of his own, his three brothers and his father's Royal Navy badges. He started as a paper boy at 14 years old in 1942, earning 25 shillings (£1.25) a week. 'I delivered newspapers and magazines to all the offices and the hospital, visiting every ward to make sure patients were served. After that, I opened the paper stall for the remainder of the morning. This was in a small hut with front lowering flap as a counter and was opposite the YMCA, on the same road as the Post Office.

'I had to cycle the two miles from West Kirby to the camp, carrying anything up to 500 papers in two bags plus magazines, books and cigarettes. Luckily, the broadsheet papers at that time were mostly only four pages! Eventually I persuaded the boss to buy a secondhand trade bike with a front carrier. I used this a lot. The Daily Mirror, price one old penny, was the most popular paper. I shall never forget a nurse telling me one day that a dying airman's request was to see Jane (the scantily-clad pin-up girl) in the Daily Mirror. I felt I had delivered some comfort.

'I closed the stall at 1pm and then returned in the evening with the evening paper, the Liverpool Echo in, at times, very bad weather. On Sunday, I delivered to The Leas (the rehabilitation centre which is described in Appendix III). Two of my sisters worked for the station. Ada, who served in the NAAFI grocery bar, has since died. Joan, who now lives in Spain, was a clerk at West Kirby Railway Station. She used to go with the station master, Mr Robinson, to the camp to issue tickets to airmen going on leave. (See Author's Note at end of this section)

'I was treated well on the camp - I had breakfast in the airmen's mess and lunch in the sergeants' mess. In the afternoons, it was tea in the officers' mess - sometimes with the Wing Commander in the kitchen. Nobody worried. I wore RAF shirts, shoes and socks and didn't have to give up clothing coupons for them. I got quite podgy with all the food. In the evenings, if it was raining, I was given a lift home, pushing my bike between the wooden seats in an RAF Bedford bus.

'During this time, I met servicemen of many nationalities, including French naval ratings with their bobble hats and later French Air Force men. Their navy blue uniforms had been bleached by the North African sun and they were issued with RAF uniforms. Poles, Czechs, Dutch and Americans came through, the latter in all their flight gear for gunnery practice. The Americans were from the Flying Fortress base at Burtonwood. Quite a few Jamaican airmen passed through the camp on arrival from the West Indies. Many of them spent time in the hospital. There were also returning British crews from Canada, mainly ground staff, in uniforms superior to our own.

'Hilbre Island was used as a decoy airfield, manned by the RAF, to deceive the German bombers which came up the Bristol Channel, then flew over the Irish Sea and over North Wales opposite the Wirral to bomb Birkenhead and Liverpool. Lights on the decoy airfield were lit by an electric generator and the generator shelter is still there.' (Another decoy site, remembered by Jim Simpson, was located in the fields between Thurstaston and Heswall. Being on the Dee side of the peninsula, it was intended to confuse enemy aircrew into believing that they were over Liverpool and the Mersey).

John Gittins recalls bombs and incendiaries being dropped in the West Kirby area. 'A smallholding was hit, along the camp road, and an old couple who lived there were killed by a landmine. This was during the time I was doing my newspaper work at West Kirby. In the time leading up to D-Day (June 6, 1944) a Spitfire crashed on a market garden near the camp. As only a skeleton staff were on the camp, the camp barber (who cut my hair) was on guard. I cycled over and gave him a Liverpool Echo to read to get a chance to sit in the Spitfire. What a thrill! The plane was upright and had only bent its propellor.'

Between his two daily deliveries, John did a little bird watching on the Saughall Massie Road. Since 1947, it has been his principal hobby and he set up the bird observatory on Hilbre island in 1957.

(Author's Note: The practice of issuing railway tickets on the camp continued. A British Railways notice from the mid-1950s, which would have been displayed on camp, listed return furlough (Forces' rate) fares to various destinations:

For the convenience of RAF personnel travelling on 48 hours leave passes, railway tickets will be booked in the NAAFI (You will be told which NAAFI by your NCO) at 6pm eachThursday night. Each Friday afternoon, railway buses will convey personnel (who have booked tickets) from the Camp Drill Shed to Liverpool to connect with main line trains from Liverpool. Return journey - Buses will return from Lime Street Station at 1.45am and 4.45am Monday morning direct to the camp.'

The list of fares (inclusive of bus travel to and from Liverpool)) included the following: Birmingham, Dudley, Wolverhampton, Sheffield, Leeds, Derby - 15 shillings (75p); Gloucester - 34 shillings (£1.70); Workington - 33 shillings (£1.65); Norwich - 59 shillings (£2.95); King's Lynn - 46 shillings and fourpence (£2.31); Ipswich - 56 shillings and twopence - (£2.80). A note at the bottom read: Only personnel booking tickets at the camp on Thursday night will be allowed to travel on Railway buses from and to the camp.)

YMCA Menu

Some of the recruits or permanent staff posted to West Kirby eventually made the area their home. 4119627 CPL BRIAN BUCK served at West Kirby from April 1953 to December 1956, working as a clerk in the equipment accounting section. He did his squarebashing at Bridgnorth. While at West Kirby he met Sheila Bond; they married in 1956 and have lived there ever since. Sheila was a helper in the YMCA hut on the camp which was run by Brom Holland and his wife Josie. 'The YMCA opened for the mid-morning break, serving cheese rolls, doughnuts and tea and soft drinks. We opened again in the evening when it was mainly tea, biscuits and soft drinks with the chance to play darts, dominoes and other games,' Sheila recalled.

(During the war there was also a YMCA canteen at what, in 2000, were the West Kirby premises of the Abbey National. A WVS canteen was located at 29 Westbourne Road. This house had been bought by Westbourne Road Methodist Church prewar and is now part of the church premises.)

He also Stayed

2589193 CPL ALLEN DOBSON, GUNNER INSTRUCTOR, an apprentice engineer who was originally from Leeds, did his squarebashing at Padgate and then a basic RAF Regiment course at Dumfries, followed by a junior gunnery instructor's course at Catterick. He came to West Kirby in January 1954 and instructed recruits in small arms use. He finished his National Service in April 1955. By this time he had met Jean Davies from Moreton at a dance in the Haig Hall in Moreton. They married and at the time of the 2000 reunion were living within two miles of the camp site.

Shear Bad Luck!

EILEEN KAVANAGH'S late husband Pat , who was a barber (he preferred the title hairdresser) at Clatterbridge Hospital, Bebington, worked three nights a week at the camp 'cutting off the RAF boys' locks' in Eileen's words. 'Most were very sad to have their lovely hair shorn off - unlike today when shaven heads are the in thing.'

Well Treated

5023326 SAC COLIN CRITTENDEN, AERO FIREMAN, squarebashed at West Kirby in June-July 1956. He enlisted with a colleague, Bryan Allen, service number 5023340. They were in Churchill Wing and are still in touch. Colin remembers how kind local people were. 'We often got into the local cinema at the cheapest prices but best seats. Once, when visiting a cafe for a cup of tea and something to eat, we

Some time in the 1950s, the Wings at West Kirby were changed from numbers 1-4 to names - Roosevelt, Smuts, Trenchard and Churchill. Winston Churchill, pictured at the controls of a Boeing 314 flying boat in January 1942, was Britain's wartime Prime Minister. (Negative No H16645)

Franklin D. Roosevelt was President of the United States from 1933 and died in April 1945, just before the end of World War II. (Negative No NYP 14413)

Marshal of the Royal Air Force Viscount Trenchard, Chief of the Air Staff 1918-29, is known as the 'Father of the RAF.' (Negative No CNA 877)

Field Marshal Jan Christian Smuts, Prime Minister of South Africa 1919-24 and 1939-48, was co-opted into Lloyd George's Cabinet in World War I. He recommended the formation of the RAF by amalgamating the Royal Flying Corps and the Royal Naval Air Service. (Negative No NYF 19627). Photos of the four leaders courtesy of the Imperial War Museum.

West Kirby, July 1956. Extreme left, standing, Colin Crittenden; extreme left, sitting, Bryan Allen; centre, sitting, Cpl Toon.

were invited to join the celebrations of a wedding party and were treated like members of the family. I guess that a uniform was still in favour, with the war still uppermost in people's memories.' Colin and Bryan both trained as firefighters at RAF Sutton-on-Hull.

From the Records

FILES at the Public Record Office contain a short history of No 5 School of Recruit Training, to give it its full title. These list many activities undertaken on and off the station, a summary of which is given below. The most impressive figure is the number of recruits trained between 1946 and 1957. The total is 155,646. The annual intake peaked at 18,751 in 1947 but, by 1957, had fallen to 10,511. The average for the 11 full years 1947-57 inclusive was over 13,500.

Officers and men carried out an ensign ceremony in Liverpool Cathedral from 1949. The ensign was presented on Battle of Britain Day in 1949 and dedicated by the Dean of the Cathedral. (A copy of the order of service for the dedication, on Sunday September 18, sent to the author by the present Dean of Liverpool, records that the ensign was given in honour of those serving in the RAF who gave their lives in the 1939-45 war. It was the gift of 1843 National Service recruits from West Kirby who had visited the cathedral between December 1947 and September 1949. Air Marshal Sir Leonard Slatter read the words of remembrance.The words of commemoration were read by Air Chief Marshal Sir Ralph Cochrane, AOC-in-C Flying Training Command, and the lesson was read by Air Marshal Sir John Baker,

AOC-in-C Coastal Command). An ensign ceremony took place at the cathedral each year, followed by a march past.

Officers and men regularly took part in the Battle of Britain service in St Bridget's Parish Church in West Kirby. Recruits and NCOs provided crowd marshalling and other help at Battle of Britain 'At Homes' at RAF Hooton Park and RAF Hawarden.

Remembrance Sunday saw contingents of 100 recruits with officers and NCOs at the war memorial at Grange Hill, with the station commander or his deputy taking the salute. Smaller contingents took part in Remembrance Day services and ceremonies at war memorials in Birkenhead, Wallasey and Hoylake and attended the Remembrance Service at Frankby Parish Church and the British Legion service in West Kirby, with the station band participating. Trumpeters were also provided for churches and Cenotaph ceremonies in Wirral and South Lancashire. Officers, NCOs and recruits took part in Civic Sunday parades in the Boroughs of Birkenhead and Wallasey and for the chairman of the council at Hoylake and in the St George's Day parade at Wallasey.

Contingents were also provided for route lining for state visits, including the following:-

May 15, 1954 - Return of the Queen from her overseas tour.
June 30, 1954 - State visit of the King and Queen of Sweden.
October 21, 1954 - Visit of the Queen to Merseyside.
April 13, 1955 - Visit of the Queen to Southport during her tour of Lancashire.
October 25-26, 1955 - State visit of the President of Portugal to London.
July 16-19, 1956 - State visit of King Feisal of Iraq to London.
June 24, 1957 - Visit of the Queen to Liverpool.
July 11, 1957 - Visit of the Queen to Wallasey. For this visit, 13 officers, 26 NCOs and 286 recruits were provided, the highest number for any of the visits listed.

Ten officers, four warrant officers, nine NCOs and 102 recruits took part in the ceremonial for the funeral of Lord Trenchard on February 20, 1956. Memorial services were also held in station churches.

Main function of the station band, composed largely of recruits and a few members of the permanent staff, was to play at the weekly passing out parade which also involved playing for the dress rehearsal the previous day. It also took part in many ceremonial parades on the station. The band's outside engagements from March to October 1957 included playing at the Electrical Contractors' Association garden fete at Llandudno; the Queen's visit to Birkenhead; The Children's Convalescent Home, West Kirby; Warrington, Widnes and District Blind People's fete at Frodsham;

Birkenhead Police fireworks display; a charity rugby match at St Helens during Battle of Britain Week; the ATC annual inspection at West Kirby; the Lord Wakefield boxing finals and No 22 Group boxing finals - both at West Kirby.

The long service records of two bandmasters are given. Flight Sgt Bowden retired, aged 65, in 1956 after 46 years continuous service (the first 12 spent in the Army). Flight Sgt McCutcheon was due to retire in 1958, aged 60, after 42 years as a bandsman and bandmaster.

Physical training and gymnastic displays are mentioned - in particular the massed movement display at Farnborough in 1950 by 400 West Kirby recruits and 400 from Bridgnorth.

Sporting achievements included: Association football - first in the Liverpool Business Houses Mid-Week League, 1954-55 season; athletics - first in No 22 Group inter-station championships, 1956-57 season; Rugby football - finalists in the RAF Inter-Station Competition (Senior Division), 1956-57 season; Shooting - winners in various inter-station competitions in 1955, 1956 and 1957; Swimming - first in No 22 Group Inter-Station Swimming Championships, 1955, 1956 and 1957; Tennis - first in the RAF Inter-Station Competition (Senior Division) 1957.

Over 1500 individuals - recruits and permanent staff - were selected for inter-service, service, command and Group events. After the introduction of the selection scheme for the commissioning of recruits in 1955, the station provided 357 candidates for further interview, 111 of whom were accepted for commissions. In 1954 the station won the Jolliffe Trophy for the best dining hall and feeding arrangements in the RAF. Three of the Station Dramatic Society's productions in the Astra Cinema, The White Sheep of the Family (March 1955), Worm's Eye View (November 1955) and The Amazing Doctor Clitterhouse (March 1956) were entered in the Command Drama Competition.

The first four airmen's married quarters were occupied on October 16, 1948. From January 1949, air experience flights lasting 20 minutes were provided for a limited number of recruits at RAF Hooton Park or RAF Hawarden but these were curtailed during the fuel crisis of late 1956. When a new training programme was introduced in September 1956, the intake and output day (i.e., the arrival and departure day for each batch of recruits) was changed from Monday to Friday.

Final entry in the short history is that on December 10, 1957, the last of 49,154 blood donors came forward, ending an association with the National Blood Transfusion Service which started on February 4, 1947.

Sheila Mercer (nee Evans) worked in the civilian post office on camp in the 1950s. She is pictured on her boss's scooter. He was the subpostmaster, Mr Freddy Johnson, who also ran the post office and shop in Newton.

Sheila's mother, Mrs Emily Evans, who also worked in the civilian post office.

Jock and Wesley. The notice gives the key to star plates on the staff cars of high-ranking officers.

Jock outside the RAF unit postal and sorting section.

Jock and Sammy who worked in the RAF post office.

The final passing out parade, on December 20, 1957, was fully reported in the Hoylake News and Advertiser dated December 27 . Reviewing officer for the parade was Air Vice-Marshal R. Faville, AOC No 22 Group. Spectators present on a cold blustery day included many Hoylake Urban District councillors with their chairman, Councillor H. Needham.

The station commander, Group Captain C.A. Watts, thanked civic dignitaries and local people for the friendliness they had shown to the station over the years. He said he regarded the station as an island surrounded by an ocean. 'We have been fortunate that our ocean is not a shark-infested one. We have met with sincerity and warmth in our friendly ocean, and for this I thank the wonderful local residents.' Some recruits had become so friendly with local residents that they had married them.

After the parade, dedication services were held in the station's Anglican and Roman Catholic chapels. An exhibition of models made by recruits during their reliability and initiative training were on view to the public and some models had been distributed in the district. A separate story in the paper records that a model of West Kirby Railway Station, made by a recruit in Trenchard Wing, had been presented to the stationmaster, Mr F. Wheatcroft. Sgt Davies is mentioned as being in charge of handicrafts and hobbies section at the camp.

The last intake, from No 2 Reception Unit at Cardington, had arrived on October 25,1957, consisting of 72 regulars and 51 National Servicemen. The numbers arriving from Cardington had been cut in August so that the station then had only two wings. From January 1958, the station was put on a care and maintenance basis. Recruits would in future go for initial training to Wilmslow and Bridgnorth. Civilian strength at the time of the closure was 19 non-industrial workers, 61 industrial; of these, 48 industrials were made redundant on January 28, 1958. The seven industrial workers with established status were absorbed in the care and maintenance establishment.

The closure report, dated January 1, 1958, lists among other details the stock of arms which was being transferred to No 16 MU (Maintenance Unit). It comprised 1463 rifles, 80 Bren guns and 65 Sten guns. At that stage, the only occupied buildings were the administrative wing site plus technical buildings and stores. The care and maintenance party were to move to the hospital site. Surplus married quarters were being declared to Air Ministry and Records Office as they became vacant. Wethersfield, where there were six vacant flats, was being cleared and would remain vacant until disposal instructions were received.

Hospital facilities ceased on December 20, 1957, and medical services would be provided in station sick quarters. Officers' sergeants' and admin. wing messes were

Site of main gate to RAF West Kirby in 2000.
(Photo Dr James D. Jones)

Aerial view of the camp site in 2000 with position of main gate marked. The uncultivated part of the site still contains the original concrete roads. This photo was taken by John Seville who was at West Kirby from May-July 1955 for squarebashing; service number 4168649. As a Junior Technician Electrics/Electronics he worked on Canberras at RAF Gutersloh, Germany.

still in operation with bulk rations being supplied to RAF Fazakerley and Haydock Park. It was not known if NAAFI facilities would remain during the care and maintenance period. The buildings were finally removed during the 1960s and part of the site returned to agriculture. The area which is accessible to the public and is crossed by several footpaths has been designated by Wirral Borough Council as an SBI (Site of Biological Importance). At the time of writing there is no plaque to mark what was once RAF West Kirby - and home to thousands of airmen.

14

History of the RAF Hospital

The Public Record Office files show that RAF West Kirby Hospital opened on May 29, 1940 - a month after the station had received its advance party (see Chapter 13). The Senior Medical Officer was Squadron Leader (Acting Wing Commander) H.C.S. Pimblett. The acting matron was Miss O. Adamson, ARRC. At this stage only No 1 Wing and No 1 MI (Medical Inspection) room had been completed. Cases of minor sickness were accommodated in two barrack huts and severe cases were evacuated to Clatterbridge General and Infectious Diseases Hospitals, Bebington, Wirral. As buildings were gradually completed, the wards were brought into use.

By December 1940, the staff comprised 12 medical officers, 25 nursing sisters and VAD (see Glossary) and one warrant officer (WO R. Taylor). Ten deaths were recorded at the hospital or on the station between September 1940 and March 1942. The records state that despite frequent air attacks from April 1940 to April 1941, no casualties were received at the camp, though slight structural damage was caused. Use was made of Thornton Manor, an EMS (Emergency Medical Services) convalescent home, owned by Viscountess Leverhulme, in February 1942. It was run on the lines of a British Red Cross establishment. (See Appendix II).

This lake now occupies the site of the hospital isolation quarters.
(Photo Ada Stewart)

97

In November 1941, 55 WAAF other ranks were substituted for 52 airmen on the hospital staff. Sister E.M. Knox was selected for WAAF welfare co-operation. In April 1943, 23 major surgical operations were carried out, 27 minor operations and 16 plasters applied.

Entertainment in February 1945 included a concert by the band of the US Army Air Force in the station cinema and an ENSA film show, This Happy Breed, in the ward. In March arrangements were made for Harland and Wolff's Employees' Association to entertain 20 patients to a football match and concert. ENSA showed the film Chip off the Old Block and discussion groups were held on different occasions.

On VE-Day, May 8 1945, when the war in Europe ended, church services were held for all personnel who wished to attend and work ceased at 10am, except for essential duties. All patients were given an issue of sweets and an extra bottle of beer. On May 15, 60 Polish airmen , who had come from Europe, arrived from RAF Wilmslow for X-ray with a further 52 on May 18. On May 28 an ambulance was sent to an air crash near The Cottage Loaf, Easley. A medical officer and orderly went; they found the pilot and passenger had received first aid and been taken to Birkenhead General Hospital.

The war in the Far East ended on August 15, 1945, and on that day (VJ-Day), there was a three-hour film show for patients, plus beer, cigarettes and sweets. Victory cakes were baked for the patients by hospital kitchen staff. Five ex-prisoners-of-war from Japan were admitted to the hospital on November 9, 1945, and then transferred to RAF Hospital Cosford.

The hospital continued to be busy, once the camp had resumed its role as a recruit training centre in 1946. The hospital had been set up as RAF West Kirby Station Hospital but in September 1950 it became RAF Hospital West Kirby, under the control of Home Command, and administered by No 63 (Western and Welsh) Group. A 'small outbreak of influenza' saw 60 cases diagnosed early in January 1953, and a further 30 admitted in the remainder of the month. In February 1953, there were 281 admissions, 233 discharges and 24 transfers. Out-patient treatments included 15 medical, 10 surgical, 19 orthopaedic, nine ENT (ear, nose and throat), 23 massage, 73 electrical, 53 exercises and 104 X-rays. Treatments for in-patients included 258 massage, 69 electrical, 511 exercises and 204 X-rays. At this time there were two beds for officers and sisters of Princess Mary's RAF Nursing Service (PMRAFNS), and 86 beds for others ranks. In addition, there were 32 beds in the Infectious Diseases Hospital.

On September 16, 1953, a variety show was given free in Ward 6 by Mr Baker and party from Hoylake. Three days later the hospital was open to visitors, with the rest of the station, for Battle of Britain Week. A free concert for patients and staff was given on October 9 by Mr Bouskill and film shows were taking place for patients every Thursday evening. Staff that month comprised seven officers, 15 PMRAFNS sisters and 15 airmen. Two reservists reported for training during the month. That year all ranks had a Christmas party and carol singers from the local YMCA visited patients. On Christmas Eve, carol singers from the camp and from the parish church visited patients. On Christmas Day patients received presents. They were visited by the station commander before their Christmas dinner and there was a concert by a station party in the evening and a film show on the evening of Boxing Day.

On May 14, 1954, a TV was installed in Ward 4 for the benefit of long-term bed cases, donated by Lord Nuffield. In December 1955, underpinning of the hospital was completed just before Christmas, except for the operating theatre floor which would take a further month to complete. It was stated that wood piles were being replaced with brick piles.

The annual inspection in 1954 was carried out by Air Commodore W.S. Hebden, AOC, and in 1956, by Air Commodore J.B.M. Wallis, AOC No 63 (Western and Welsh) Group. In February 1957, Flying Officer Holland made several visits in connection with the investigation of respiratory infections during 1956-57.

The hospital OC was in charge of medical arrangements when a one-week exercise was held in January 1956 at No 1 Personnel Dispatch Unit (Author's Note: This was, presumably, a remnant of the station's function as a Personnel Dispatch Centre during the war). The exercise, with 330 recruits taking the place of reservists, was 'to evaluate the problems associated with the task of converting a School of Recruit Training into a Personnel Dispatch Unit within the timescale of current mobilisation instructions.' For the purpose of the exercise, items of tropical kit, which were to be issued, would be simulated by the issue of appropriate items of blue. In the event of war, M-Day was mobilisation day; the PDU would start to operate at M-Day plus 6. The closure arrangements for the camp in December 1957 stated that No 1 Personnel Dispatch Unit was to be withdrawn from the PDU organisation and equipment stored at West Kirby for PDU purposes disposed of.

By December 20, 1957, staff had fallen to six officers, two PMRAFNS sisters and 35 other ranks. In the three weeks to that date, there were 15 admissions, 27 discharges and one transfer. Six in-patients and ten out-patients received physiotherapy; four in-patients and 21 out-patients were X-rayed. The hospital closed on January 1, 1958.

One of the medical officers who had connections with the hospital was Acting Squadron Leader J.P. McCrory. He was at West Kirby from 1953-55 and was officer in charge of Station Medical Sick Quarters. The medical centre was then in a Nissen hut. His title was later changed to Senior Medical Officer of the station. Recalling those days, he said: 'I enjoyed looking after the recruits.'

Any of his patients needing more attention than the medical centre could give were sent to the station hospital where, from time to time, he was duty medical officer. Otherwise, his duties were entirely on the station. Off-duty, Squadron Leader McCrory was a keen member of Hoylake Rugby Club. He played for them regularly and also persuaded some people from the station to turn out for the club. He left the RAF in 1968 after 16 years' service and became a GP in Norwich, finally retiring in 1983.

Dream Posting

DR JAMES D. JONES, service number 2340652 and known to all his friends as Pip, was called up in January 1947 and came to West Kirby as an AC1 medical orderly to work in the hospital. It was a dream posting as his parents lived only a mile from the main gate in the village of Greasby. He hoped to stay there for the rest of his service. However, he was promoted to LAC and posted to the Middle East in early 1948, eventually remustering and becoming a sergeant in the education branch. After demob, he qualified as a doctor and later became a GP in Oxton, Birkenhead.

Dr Jones recalls that the rifle range at West Kirby was used by the Home Guard during the war. 'Local amateur gangs of thieves would invade the range to recover spent ammunition to sell as scrap metal.' In the hospital, a high percentage of patients were admitted with rheumatic fever - 'a serious condition that could lead to chronic health problems in later life to heart, kidney and other body systems. It could start from a simple illness, such as a sore throat but was made worse by cold, damp and lack of heating fuel. The winter of 1947 was the worst for 60 years. This was compounded by a shortage of coal and coke to heat the large cold, damp barrack huts. Toilet and sewerage water froze and pipes burst.'

Flying Hopes Dashed

HIS stay in the hospital in 1949 marked the end of 3119372 AC2 JOHN BEASLEY'S ambition of a flying career in the RAF. John had already passed his aircrew medical and intelligence tests and was looking forward to starting flying training, hopefully as a pilot, at RAF Sealand after completing his final two weeks' squarebashing at West Kirby.

His troubles began on a Sunday afternoon, May 1, 1949, almost at the end of a roller-skating session in Liverpool, with his pal Irving Bolant from Huddersfield.

He had the sensation of a sprained left ankle. Plans to have tea in Liverpool and take a look at the city were abandoned. Instead, it was back to West Kirby by train and a taxi to camp. 'The walk from the main gate was very painful and I was extremely pleased to see my bed. Irving knew about first aid and administered a cold water bandage. Sleep that night was just a series of naps.

Dennis Brooks, medical orderly.

Top
Johnny Chick with Sister Quigley outside Ward 6.

Bottom
Left to right, Frank, blood count man; Tony, medical orderly; Johnny Chick. The photo is looking towards the junction of the corridor and Ward 6.

(All Photos on this page via John Beasley)

'All through the night I was restless. I could feel something happening to my joints. At reveille the climax came. I could not move without an excruciating pain in both ankles, knees and wrists. Cpl Titherington was called, then Sgt Woodhouse. He detailed another airman to help Irving dress me and give me a rifle carriage (being carried on two rifles used as a stretcher) to the wing guardroom. A waiting ambulance took me to the hospital. I was taken on a stretcher to the almoner's office and lowered gently to the floor. After a quick examination he said 'Ward 6.' Sister was waiting for me and I was put in a bed just past her office.

'The MO, a squadron leader, came shortly and called me by my Christian name. He told me I had acute rheumatic fever and put me on 4 grammes sodium solicylate (soda sal) every four hours with two very small white tablets. I was to have a blood count every Monday morning. My blood count was 140; it should have been 4. For the next month I was competely oblivious to all the other patients in the ward. The medical orderly, who had just been posted to West Kirby, Dennis Brooks, took good care of me.

'I expected to stay in hospital a month but I was there for nine months. Other patients came and spoke to me. There was a very warm atmosphere in the ward and, as patients got better, they would help the male nurses and the sister in limited ways. Breakfast came on a large trolley, usually collected by a patient who was ready to leave hospital. After breakfast came the medicine trolley. Sister was in charge so there was no avoiding it. My medicine was the most vile I have ever tasted.

'Next came Frank from the haematology department with his trolley, with an impressive display of small phials, needles, cottonwool and instruments. He was always cheerful and we were all keen to know how our blood was doing. Mid-morning we had tea, a biscuit and Housewives' Choice on the radio. By the end of the first month, most of the other patients had come to see me as I was 'strict flat bed' apart from a small pillow, about three inches thick.

'John Chick, my immediate neighbour, who came from Lyme Regis, could cheer up any patient feeling depressed. Depression was very serious and could lead to patients throwing away their medicine. Few of us had visitors - an exception was Sidney Lunt who came from Liverpool.

Monthly film shows helped to raise morale. Beds were moved and the heads raised so that those patients who were strict bed could see the screen.

'Late on Saturday afternoons, a Salvation Army member, who was at least six feet tall, regularly cycled to the hospital from West Kirby, bringing gramophone records which had been requested and also the local newspaper and the Liverpool Echo. He would stay for about four hours, taking orders for anything a patient wanted and he could get. The handicraft trolley came once a week and patients, even while flat on their backs, were encouraged to do things like embroidery.

'Cocoa came at 10pm. The only way I could taste it was to drink it without sugar or milk - such was the effect of the soda sal. During my fourth month, I developed a painful infection in the right ear (otorrhoea). The treatment, equally painful, was to be turned on the left side and have Acriflavine drops inserted. I developed a rash across my middle during the hot summer months. Sister Quigley prescribed Wakefield ointment, rather like a vapour rub or Russian tallow, for this. It burned but was effective. A cabinet in the ward contained small bottles of Guinness - one per day for those who wanted it.'

Other friends John recalls from the hospital were John Galpin from Portsmouth; John Dansie, London; George Gale, Kent; Richard Boaz, London; Robert Deakin, London; Roy Barclay, Kent. To his great regret, John was medically discharged from the RAF in January 1950 and resumed his apprenticeship as a printer. He has continued a link with the RAF through the RAF Association and is currently standard bearer for the Twickenham branch.

Lots of Bull

3108314 CPL ANDREW DEWAR, NURSING ORDERLY, was posted to the hospital in March 1948 and stayed until demobbed in October 1949. Apart from a short time at No 2 MI (Medical Inspection) room, he spent his service in various wards. He recalls the surgical ward which catered for minor operations, the general medical ward, another devoted to rheumatic fever ('which always seemed to be full'), an isolation ward which was separate at the back of the hospital, a ward for officers and the X-ray department. Dental work was also carried out.

Sister Scott, July 1949.
(Photo via Andrew Dewar)

Andrew Dewar in Meols,
August 1949.
(Photo via Andrew Dewar)

'Compared with hospitals today, we seemed to have a much harder time. Ward floors had to be polished daily which meant all beds on one side of the ward being moved to the other side, the polish applied and the shine brought up by swinging a heavy weight covered in cloth from side to side. This was repeated on the other side. Daily ward inspections by the sister and matron meant a lot of bull and this was stepped up for the weekly inspection by the MO.

'We worked three different shifts - 0800 to 1700; 0800 to 2000, with three hours, 1400 to 1700 off duty; and 2000 to 0800. It was normal, on the second shift, to walk through the fields to Hoylake where there was a grand cafe which served cream teas. We didn't seem to get to West Kirby very much as it was quicker to walk to Meols Station when going to Liverpool on leave.'

Brawls and Falls

2515197 SAC ACTING CORPORAL FRED BRANDWOOD, NURSING ATTENDANT, really enjoyed his time as a ward master at the hospital from September 1951-April 1953. At that time there were 12 wards. Fred's duties were all administration - booking patients in to the hospital, typing medical records, issuing travel warrants when patients were due for discharge back to their respective units, if outside the West Kirby area. He was 21 and married when he arrived at the hospital. He never lived on camp as he had a living-out pass - 'it was home for me when my shift ended.' His shifts were mornings, afternoons or nights but no weekend duties.

'Night shift required us to link up with the night sister as to the number of patients in residence at 23.59 hours and the number to be discharged next morning. Night duty was at its busiest on Thursdays after passing out parade. This was the direct result of brawls and falls after the celebrations in the local hostelries. We also had a few suicide attempts, both from recruits and from married quarters, but thankfully no fatalities in my time. (Author's Note: Files seen by the author record only one suicide - of an AC2 in March 1956. Cause of death was strangulation by asphyxiation. He had been found dead in the ablution block. The verdict at the inquest was 'Suicide while the balance of the mind was disturbed.')

'The night duty medical officer was a sleeping duty. The Senior Medical Officer was Wing Commander Rice and the other senior staff were Squadron Leader Robinson, Medical Officer; Flight Lieutenant Lennard, Medical Officer; and the matron - a Squadron Officer whose name I can't recall. There were six ward sisters - all Flight Officers - plus nursing attendants. Hospital Warrant Officer Carolyn, the oldest man on camp, had joined the Royal Flying Corps as a boy entrant in World War I.

'Flight Sgt Wignold, Cpl Jones and myself comprised the nursing admin staff. In the hospital kitchen, a sergeant, corporal and airmen attended to the dietary needs of patients. The cleaners were civilians who lived locally. The main medical conditions dealt with were chest problems. TB was rife at that time. Minor surgery was carried out - tonsillectomies, bad cuts, haemorrhoids, foot problems etc. All sexually-transmitted disease cases were transferred to RAF Hospital Cosford.'

TB Patient

3516187 LAC JIM SIMPSON, AIRFRAME MECHANIC, did his squarebashing at West Kirby in 1953 (see Chapter 13). He had signed on for four years regular service in the RAF and after three years came back to West Kirby and spent six months in the TB (tuberculosis) ward of the hospital. He was admitted to Ward 4 in May 1956 and much of his early treatment consisted of bed rest plus four months chemotherapy. After this, Jim was still on a strict regime. He was allowed up for one hour per day (first week), two hours (second week), and finally to a maximum of six hours per day, when home leave was allowed.

*Visiting time.
The patient is Cpl Jim
Barrowman. His wife
Kath, a local Hoylake
girl, is on the right*
(Photo Jim Simpson)

*Two patients.
Left, Eddy Reihl; centre,
Cpl Wallace Powell. The
name of the PMRAFNS
sister is not known. (Photo
Jim Simpson)*

Ward 4 patients doing exercises under the supervision of a white-coated physiotherapist. Left, Colin Taylor; centre, Phil Kilshaw; right, not known.
(Photo Jim Simpson)

Ward 4 interior. The bottles were the daily ration, in Jim Simpson's time, of one bottle of Mackeson's stout!
(Photo Jim Simpson)

He was confined to the hospital up to and throughout the period of being allowed up for four hours per day. When he had passed the 'magic' four-hour stage, he was allowed out of camp. The nursing sisters were PMRAFNS officers and many of the orderlies were National Servicemen.

He remembers three of the sisters on Ward 4 - Sister Butler, who was ward sister, Sister Gumley, who was Scottish, and Sister Klupsch. Because the number of TB cases in the country was going down, a number of specialised TB hospitals had closed and Ward 4 housed some civilian patients. The service patients came from all over the UK and abroad.

By that stage, there were no operating facilities in the hospital and patients who needed operations were sent to Broadgreen Hospital in Liverpool. In October 1956, Jim spent three weeks at the Collaton Cross rehabilitation centre, Newton Ferrers in Devon. It was a multi-service centre at that time and Jim was billeted with Royal Marine commandos, most of whom had been injured in climbing accidents. Jim was invalided out of the RAF in early 1957, a few months before he was due to be demobbed. (His wartime memories are given in Chapter 13).

Creepy Place

CPL KEN RIMELL, PHOTOGRAPHIC TECHNICIAN, went to West Kirby in 1959, well after it had ceased to be a recruit training centre. He was on a photographer's course and the old hospital buildings were opened up for people on the course. 'We used the medical section to process films and prints. It was a very creepy place - very forbidding - and I was glad to get away from it.' Ken subsequently worked in the Air Investigation Branch and, for the last two years of his service, worked in the newly-formed Public Relations Department. This helped him prepare for his civilian career as a Press photographer.

Where is West Kirby?

MOST of the 155,000 recruits who travelled to West Kirby between 1946 and 1957 were going to a place they had never visited and had only heard of from other RAF personnel who had been there before. If they were like me, they learned little about the town in their eight or ten-week stay. After leaving the camp, they were unlikely to return.

So what kind of place is West Kirby? Guide books contain only brief entries about the town, among them the following.

West Kirby - 'a Wirral resort and residential district at the mouth of the River Dee with good bathing and sands.' - AA Illustrated Road Book of England and Wales 1962.

West Kirby - 'seaside town overlooking Hilbre Island (once an important telegraph station) and the mountains of Wales. There is known to have been a church at 'Cherchbie' before the Norman Conquest.' - The Shilling Guide, published by Shell-Mex and BPO 1964. Hilbre Island was a cell of Chester Abbey until the Dissolution of the Monasteries by Henry VIII according to Pevsner and Hubbard's The Buildings of England.

Merseyside saw vast industrial development in the 19th century, creating thousands of jobs in shipbuilding and other industries. The population of Wirral grew - the civil parish of West Kirby expanded from 1118 in 1881 to 2441 in 1891. By 1951, it had reached almost 18,000.

The coming of the railways was a key factor in the growth of the area, providing quick and easy transport to Birkenhead and Liverpool. According to Pevsner, the railway was extended from Hoylake in 1878 and a link with Liverpool was established in 1888. A History of Cheshire by Alan Crosby gives these details about the growth of the railways:-

'The Hoylake Railway, opened from Birkenhead in 1866, had so little traffic that in 1870 it went bankrupt but in 1883, the Wirral Railway Company was formed and after taking over the Hoylake line, operated a short network linking West Kirby, New Brighton, Seacombe and Birkenhead Park.

'The company ran an intensive suburban service, with frequent trains, closely spaced stations and regular interval timetables, and its value was greatly increased after 1886 when the Mersey Railway opened the first tunnel between Liverpool Central, Tranmere and Birkenhead Park'.

In 1935 the lines from Birkenhead to West Kirby and New Brighton were electrified. The present electric service between Liverpool and West Kirby is operated by Merseyrail. The station nearest to the RAF camp site is Meols. (Author's Note: I travelled back from there after my visit to West Kirby in March 2000. In fact, Meols was the only village I could remember in the West Kirby area.)

In my research, I have picked up glimpses of the wartime history of the district. Camouflage nets were made in a house called Broomfields in Hoylake, which was requisitioned for war work. Nets were hung on large wooden frames and the women workers, wearing cotton masks to protect their noses and mouths from powder on the long strips of hessian which had to be threaded between the nets.

There was a rehabilitation centre for injured aircrew at The Leas School, a private school in Meols Drive, Hoylake (see Appendix III).

The name of West Kirby has spread far and wide. John L. Lockett, writing in The Wirral Journal No 8, Spring 1997, says that in 30 years of travelling both at home

Meols Station, nearest railway station to the RAF camp, in 2000.
(Photo: Dr James D. Jones)

and abroad, the only people he met who had heard of West Kirby were ex-RAF personnel. He recalls meeting a Boeing 747 captain in Bahrain who remembered West Kirby with loathing; a consul at the British Embassy in Peking who shuddered when he read John Lockett's address; and a toolmaker in South Africa who twitched when West Kirby was mentioned.

Mr Lockett adds: 'All the scores of men I have spoken to recalled the harsh treatment they had endured as National Servicemen when under training at West Kirby. Paradoxically, they all stated that this gruelling period of their lives had been beneficial to them.'

His schoolboy memories include seeing recruits in shorts, singlets, thick socks and boots marching to the crossroads at Newton. 'Until the DIs gave the order 'For-ward', the red-faced, agonised, sweating airmen would double mark time, bringing their knees up hip high to the accompaniment and shouts from the DIs... They would set off for Caldy at a brisk pace with the DIs effortlessly shouting out the timing from their sturdy RAF issue bicycles.'

John Lockett recalls waving to airmen in canvas-covered Bedford and Foden trucks as he and his brother waited for the school bus; hearing the crack of rifles and the chatter of Bren guns from the firing range and never tiring of hearing the 'melodious, yet stirring sound of the RAF March Past.'

At Evensong in Frankby Church, the congregation would be swelled by numerous trainees in their No 1 uniform ('best blue'). 'They always looked subdued but sang the hymns with gusto. On Christmas Eve, the church choir would visit the camp hospital to sing carols to the airmen who were too ill or injured to go home for the festive season.

'I will always remember how beautiful and angelic the female nurses looked wearing their starched headdresses and cloaks. Afterwards the camp's catering staff would lay on an Epicurean feast for us. I doubt that the conscripts received such fare.'

(Author's Note: The telegraph station on Hilbre Island was built in 1841 as part of a chain of visual signalling stations linking Holyhead with Liverpool. The nurses referred to in the paragraph above were in fact the sisters - officers serving in Princess Mary's RAF Nursing Service.)

Appendix II

Thornton Manor, the home of Viscountess Leverhulme, was used as an Emergency Medical Services Convalescent Home in the Second World War (see Chapter 8). The author has not been able to trace any records of the home at that time. However, Unilever Historical Archives have made available a copy of an article which appeared in Port Sunlight News, the Port Sunlight house magazine, for July 1940. It describes a fete held at Thornton Manor in aid of the Red Cross and Comforts Fund (Mayoress of Bebington's Appeal). It recalls the spirit of the period and permission has been given for it to be reproduced in full. The Prime Minister referred to in the article was Winston Churchill. Admiral Sir Edward Evans commanded HMS Broke, a destroyer serving with the Dover Patrol in World War I. According to Paul Kemp in the book Sea Warfare, on the night of April 20-21, 1917, in company with HMS Swift, his ship fought a spirited engagement with six German destroyers in which two of the German ships were sunk. After this, he was known as 'Evans of the Broke.' Mr Herbert Morrison, also referrred to in the article, was Minister of Supply. The article appears below.

THORNTON MANOR FETE
To aid Red Cross and Comforts Fund

As a result of the Fete and Country Fair held at Thornton Manor on the last Saturday in June, the Red Cross and Comforts Fund (Mayoress of Bebington's Appeal) will benefit to an amount of about £900. The gross receipts exceeded £1100 and all who contributed, every helper, and the five thousand who attended the fete, deserve thanks for their share in this splendid result. The Mayoress of Bebington (Mrs F. McLeavy) and Lady Leverhulme worked indefatigably for its success, and they are most grateful to all who assisted them.

It was a great pleasure to have at the opening ceremony Admiral Sir Edward Evans, of whom members of the United Comrades Federation have happy recollections as the speaker at their annual dinner a few years ago. Lady Evans accompanied him, and among others present were the Mayor and Mayoress of Bebington, the Mayor and Mayoress of Birkenhead (Alderman W.H. and Miss S. Egan), Colonel Sir John Shute, Mr and Mrs Graham White and Capt Alan Graham, MP.

Admiral and Lady Evans were welcomed by Lord Leverhulme, who presided at the opening ceremony. To introduce the first-named, he said, was a simple task, for he just had to say 'Evans of the Broke,' and that sufficed. Sir Edward was now engaged on organizing the defence of aircraft factories throughout the country. He welcomed particularly Lady Evans, because she was a native of Norway, and their hearts went out to the people of her country. He paid a tribute to the work of the various committees responsible for the Fair.

Admiral Evans, in referring to the war and Britain's attitude to it, spoke in high terms of our Prime Minister. In travelling about the country, Sir Edward had sensed among the people a magnificent spirit - the spirit of the bulldog. The country was not now relying entirely on its three fighting forces, he said, but also on the factory workers and the numerous other services engaged on home defence. Almost alone, but with the valuable aid of our Colonies, we faced the enemy. We had a Cabinet composed of members of all political parties, and we presented a common front. Every one of us was a serving member, and it was British character that was going to win the war. 'I wish you lots of luck, and, as Mr Herbert Morrison says, 'Go to it.'

A warm vote of thanks was accorded Sir Edward and Lady Evans, on the motion of the Mayor of Bebington, seconded by Lady Leverhulme. Later, Admiral Evans reviewed The Boys' Brigade and the Sea Guides.

The Market and Fair

The various events, the donors of gifts, and the names of all the helpers are too numerous to report in detail, as space is limited, but it is fitting to mention here that Port Sunlight contributed its quota in no small degree.

The Country Market found many willing purchasers at the various stalls. There were cakes, produce, hardware and pottery, a garden stall, sweets and tobacco, groceries, a 'Men's Own Stall' by the Vinolia Company, and a Grand Lucky Dip.

The Fun Fair attractions, which were many and varied, were organized by members of Port Sunlight clubs. There was boxing, too. Second-Lieut. Jack Peterson (the former boxing champion) refereed a number of bouts between members of an Army boxing team and the Port Sunlight Boxing Club.

Such occasions are invariably enhanced by music, and an excellent programme was presented by the Band of the M.G.T.C. Cheshire Regiment (by kind permission of Lt.-Colonel B.Y. Hayes-Newington).

The Gorseacre Stage Society and the Port Sunlight Players each gave enjoyable concerts, while a popular feature was the Grand Talent Competition. A Grand Concert came as a finale to the proceedings, and this was held in the Ball Room, where there were presented the prizes won in the numerous draws which had been held to help the cause. By the way, three were unclaimed - pink ticket 491 (cushion), white ticket 66C (coffee table), and purple ticket 475 (d'oyleys) (sic) - and if any readers hold these, they should apply at once to the Lever Library.

Appendix *III*

High Jinks at The Leas

NEARLY 3000 airmen, injured and broken in their duties, treated in three years, and of that number the amazing proportion of 82½ per cent restored to flying duties. This is the opening paragraph of a story published in the Liverpool Daily Post in 1944. The place where all this happened was The Leas, Meols Drive, Hoylake - a wartime orthopaedic rehabilitation centre for NCO aircrew and others. Because of censorship, the newspaper account could only identify it as 'a centre in the North-West.'

It describes the centre, officially known as No 2 Airmen's Convalescent Depot, as 'a place to which men come who have had limbs broken and expertly mended to be brought back to as near 100 per cent of their pre-accident fitness as possible.' Then comes this tribute: 'That so many should have been able to resume flying; that only 2¼ per cent should have been invalided out, is the finest possible tribute to a centre whose methods have been copied all over the country.'

The report continues: 'First then, the primary surgery, which Squadron Leader (Harold) Cantor, Liverpool-trained orthopaedic surgeon who has been in medical charge here since the opening , insists has been magnificent. 'We only complete the job they do so brilliantly,' he says modestly.

'Secondly, the facilities for the work, provided by the Commanding Officer, Wing Commander G.W. Dawes, DSO, who has also been here from the beginning. First the men are given surroundings as happy as it is possible to make them. Sunny bedrooms, delightfully furnished recreation rooms, good food, well cooked, and every facility for recreation. Then the remedial facilities: gymnasia, a swimming-bath, workshops, playing-fields.

'Working to a scientific schedule, but all within a sort of holiday camp atmosphere, instructors work all day teaching men to walk again, to use their arms, to bend backs that have just come out of plaster jackets.' One of the instructors was Edmund Burke, a prewar Davis Cup tennis coach. Among the patients receiving treatment at this time was Warrant Officer Thomas Parrington, who before the war had raced cars on Birkdale sands. He had baled out of an aircraft 14,000 feet above the North Sea. His parachute failed to open with the ripcord and in opening it by hand, the cords bent an arm back and broke both that and his neck. He landed in a gorse bush and, in trying to get away, fell into a limepit. He was found and taken to hospital.

Several former patients and one ex-medical officer at The Leas have contacted the author of this book and their stories are given below.

Dr Nick Hughes, who qualified in medicine at Liverpool University in 1942, joined the RAF in January 1943. After a few months as MO to a squadron in Bomber Command, he was posted to The Leas as a flight lieutenant. He recalls that the CO, Wing Commander Dawes, was a veteran navigator of World War I. He flew as 17, which Dr Hughes believes means that he was the 17th commissioned officer in the Royal Flying Corps. Dr Hughes' experience confirms the high rate of success of The Leas. 'We swam, played squash and golf with patients and got them back - about 85 per cent of them - to flying duties. Some of the patients slept at The Royd and other of the big houses adjacent to The Leas.'

The civilian in charge of orthopaedic services in the RAF was the distinguished orthopaedic surgeon, Reginald Watson-Jones, later knighted for his services to the RAF in this field. Ten orthopaedic units of 100-150 beds were set up in strategically placed RAF hospitals and these were backed up by the residential rehabilitation centres. Watson-Jones visited them all monthly. As well as using their professional skill, each member of the teams in the hospitals and rehabilitation centres had to possess a confident, cheerful personality which would inculcate in the patients the will to get well and not allow apathy to develop. Sir Reginald died in 1972.

A letter from Sir Reginald at the end of 1944, thanked Dr Hughes for his hard work over the previous year. He was posted to the rehabilitation unit at Loughborough University in December 1944 and later, as a squadron leader, went to start another rehabilitation unit at Collaton Cross near Newton Ferrers, Devonshire. He played rugger for Waterloo and post-war for Leicester, playing against New Zealand three times and against Australia. He finished as president of Leicester Tigers.

Journey by Boneshaker

FLT SGT DAVID HOPKINS was a flight engineer on a Halifax bomber, carrying out 12-hour meteorological patrols over the Atlantic. He relates his experiences.

On D-Day, June 6, 1944, his aircraft crashed into the sea 750 miles from Great Britain. The crew were picked up on the third day by an American anti-submarine patrol and landed in the USA. On return to England, David passed through West Kirby, in its role as a transit camp, before rejoining his squadron, 517, at Brawdy in South-west Wales. He takes up the story.

'On returning from a met patrol on August 27, 1944, we ran into thick fog blanketing our airfield and, running low on petrol after 12 hours flying, couldn't meet the

114

diversion request. Due to barometric pressure changes, our altimeter was inaccurate and we hit the top of a mountain. This resulted in a compound fracture of my left leg.

'I was taken to a small village hospital in Haverfordwest and given six pints of blood. The compound fracture was perfectly aligned by the medical staff. The RAF considered the work we were doing was classified, so they sent an ambulance to collect me. The ambulance, being a military vehicle with no mod cons, was a real boneshaker - and it did just that. It jolted my broken bones out of alignment.

'I was taken to the RAF General Hospital at Church Village, near Pontypridd, South Wales. My leg was put into traction, but unfortunately the traction pin was not sterile and caused an infection in my knee. Penicillin cured the problem but the femur was set out of alignment and my knee would not bend. When the wounds healed, I was sent to The Leas for physiotherapy to try to get my knee back to normal.

'Physical training and exercise was the order of the day to get the injured limbs and muscles back into good working order. There was a small hydrotherapy pool at The Leas which was very good for the manipulation of stiff joints. At the far side of the playing field was a heated swimming pool which was stoked by some New Zealand aircrew to steaming point. It was the first and only time I have swum in hot water and it was very exhilarating. There were no swimming costumes, so skinny dipping was the order of the day, and in those days men were men.

'Although food was rationed, we seemed to be blessed with an abundance. We paid a nominal weekly mess fee and a local farm, probably from under the counter, supplied plenty of bacon and eggs. With the eggs the cooks produced a variety of cakes and other goodies. Being classed as hospital patients, we had to wear light blue uniforms and red ties. There was also a night curfew set at 10 pm.

'Many airmen broke the curfew and sneaked back in via the golf course at the rear of The Leas. One in particular, Tommy Morgan, a Scotsman, had a girl friend in Hoylake and was always sneaking back into the dormitory in the early hours, disturbing everybody. To get our own back, on one occasion, we put a hedgehog in his bed. Apart from the shock of climbing into bed in the dark, hedgehogs are lousy.

'On another occasion, we suspended his bed from the rafters so that it swung like a hammock. It didn't cure him, but it cost him a fortune in matches. I can still see him striking them every night to check his bed.

'A large number of Canadian and Australian aircrew were undergoing treatment. They had a cavalier attitude to rules and regulations (Eat drink and be merry - tomorrow is another day.) They had a bad habit of bringing back souvenirs after a night out on the town, much to the consternation of the admin staff. The long ornate mirror over the washbasins was a trophy from a local pub.

'They would annoy the wealthy residents of Meols Drive by pinching their gates and dumping them down side roads. They acquired large tins of paint (where from, during the war?) and poured the paint in stripes, like a rainbow, down the main road. Their antics, I believe, led to the premature closing of the establishment. Whenever the police arrived after an incident, there was much bed-hopping, like the best film comedies, to show a full complement of patients accounted for.

'A very popular Cockney sergeant physiotherapist, Johnny Bush, was on guard duty one evening when a gang of Aussies arrived very late (about midnight - two hours after curfew) and came into the guard room. They said: 'Johnny, we've brought you a present.' He had visions of fish and chips or beer. They said: 'We've left it on the forecourt.' They promptly disappeared before he had time to book them. He went out and there on the drive was a bumper car. It could only have come from Moreton Shore or New Brighton where there were fairgrounds. Did they buy or steal it? How did they manage to push it all the way back in the dark, taking turns in pushing and steering? No mean feat.

Fearing that it had been unlawfully acquired, and fearful of the subsequent repercussions, Johnny Bush dashed into the building and dragged two PT corporals out of bed. They pushed, dragged and carried the bumper car on to the Royal Liverpool Golf Course (hallowed ground) and buried it before daylight. Some day, someone with a metal detector will think they've found buried treasure. But I wouldn't be surprised, judging by Johnny Bush's language, if they didn't find a couple of Aussies buried with it.

'On the good side, was the esteem given to aircrew by the public in general and the many invitations we received. I had free tickets to the matinees at most Liverpool theatres. Parties and wedding receptions were quite common. I accepted an invitation to a works dance and met my wife there. I got to like Wirral so much that I put down my roots here. So I have to be grateful to the RAF for sending me to The Leas to recuperate.'

David Hopkins spent a long time in hospitals during and after the war before his leg and knee movement recovered to a tolerable degree. He was subsequently discharged from the RAF with a 70 per cent leg disability. His hospital experiences stood him in good stead and he made his career in the NHS, ultimately becoming district engineer for North Wirral with responsibility for 12 hospitals. His two daughters are ward sisters and his son is a hospital consultant.

Only Survivor

FRANK MUNRO, a sergeant wireless operator, was thrown out of a Wellington bomber which crashed in the Middle East on June 23, 1944. He had joined the RAF at the end of 1942 and was sent to Blackpool for squarebashing on the streets plus four hours Morse code training each day. In May, he went to Yatesbury, Wiltshire, to build up higher Morse speeds and in August practice in the air, first in De Havilland Rapides and then in Percival Proctors. He remembers the Rapide pilot who used to read the Daily Mirror while flying and the one who used to dive down and 'shoot up' Land Girls working in the fields.

By the end of November, he was a trained wireless operator and entitled to wear an 'S', standing for Signaller, brevet (badge) on his uniform. As no S brevets were available, he and his colleagues blocked out part of the B on a bomb aimer's brevet to make a rough S and had these sewn on. 'The best thing were the sergeant's stripes - and the ten shillings and sixpence (52½p) pay per day. I travelled into Chippenham with a couple of other lads and celebrated in a small teahouse on Welsh Rarebit .' Frank went on ten days embarkation leave just before Christmas. Early in January, he landed at Port Said in Egypt, did a two-week gunnery course at El Balah on the edge of the Suez Canal and then to Jerusalem for two weeks training on American Bendix radio equipment. He and his colleagues hoped they would be flying in B24 Liberators but instead were put on, in Frank's words, clapped out Wellingtons.

'After a while, we liked them and were still on them when I was posted to Italy in June 1944. On the night flight before leaving, we were recalled because of fog and crashed at 2.25am on June 24. We flew into the ground. I was thrown out in the crash and received serious leg injuries but the others all died.

'I was returned to England in a hospital ship, spent five months in the EMS (Emergency Medical Services) hospital at Wharncliffe, Sheffield. In February 1945 I was sent to The Leas and spent three periods there. On arrival at The Leas, I was told to find a bed space in hut No 2. The huts so-called were very clean, painted inside and out in off-white. The beds were set well apart with a mat on the floor between each bed, a tall locker as well as small locker, where one could place a photograph of either your girl friend or wife (very few, if any, were married). The beds had hospital-type blankets with a blue counterpane over them. Civilian staff kept the place clean and made the beds for us.

'Each of the huts was connected by a long continuous corridor on one side. The entrance to each hut was offset, opposite were the toilets and bathrooms. The huts were quite close to the gym, which helped when it rained, likewise the house itself. There was a small NAAFI where each morning during tea break there would be a frantic rush to obtain newspapers and then wait for the first chap to shout out he had completed the crossword.

'War news was ignored, the crossword was the most important item in the paper. The New Zealand lads were very good at doing these; they took great pleasure in telling us they had a better education in New Zealand! We also had quite a few cribbage players who used to play at every opportunity. Some would even play before we went to the gym each morning on parade.

'The house had a large dining room with wood panelling round most of the room to a height of four feet. Above this on the walls on one side were framed photographs of various airmen who had won the VC. The tables in this room were of good quality with chairs which seated eight or ten at each sitting. We were waited on by WAAFs which was an enormous help for those who had difficulty in walking. The food was good most of the time.

'The rest of the ground floor of the house was taken up by offices, treatment rooms, games room, reading and writing room. The day after arrival, we were individually seen and checked over by Squadron Leader Cantor and assigned to whichever group and PT instructor we should join. A fixed number of hours were spent in the gym each day and in the school grounds.

'Some of the PT instructors (all sergeants) were billeted next door in the Golf Club with other members of staff. They were good at their job, older than most of us and two or three of them had been professional footballers in Civvy Street. They had to be good to be posted to The Leas where a high standard had to be maintained with each of them being able to motivate us to work hard at our exercises, become fit and if possible become one of the few who on a Monday morning in the gym would have his name called out from 'The Chop List' - meaning, return to unit or squadron if he could be used again for operational flying.

'With the few Commonwealth lads I find it difficult to recall any instance of ill-feeling of any sort, in spite of the differences in background, country of origin or degree of experience of each individual. It had been the same on the flying side: it helped to add colour and character to our way of life because, for a great many of us, it was indeed a short life.

'We had the odd bod who on arrival would start to shoot a line of how it had been for him. In our hut we had a lad from Glasgow who was really a quiet and unassuming person. 'Jock' (all Scots were called Jock) would move and stand before the stove at his end of the hut and say in a loud voice: 'Have I ever told you about my seventh trip to Berlin?' Instant silence would fall; nobody could survive that number of trips to the big city - seven - ye gods! Most of us were well aware that Jock had been there and back that number of times. This was a subtle way to shut the newcomer up and was nearly always successful.

'Early in March, a small number of aircrew arrived at The Leas who had been repatriated from German prisoner-of-war camps because of their wounds. They had either been shot up by German night fighters or flak or still been in the kite when it crashed and been injured then. On arrival in the UK, they were all sent to hospital for a medical check and to receive any necessary treatment. After leave, they reported to The Leas.

'Most had lost part of one leg, either above or below the knee. Most arrived wearing weird and strange contraptions that enabled them to walk. These were fashioned and made from coffee and syrup tins and bits and pieces of metal. The tins had come from Red Cross parcels sent to the camps as part of a food supplement. In the mess, we noticed they ate everything the WAAFs put before them.

'Within days they were sent, usually in pairs, by train to Roehampton Hospital, just south of London, where they stayed for a few days to have artificial limbs made and fitted. At this late stage of the war, people were starting to return to the Hoylake area for Easter holidays and incredibly complaints started to come in about men in white jumpers and, if the weather was warm enough, shorts, riding bicycles around Hoylake and as far as Wallasey and New Brighton. Some of them had only one leg, said the complainants, and an instructor was shouting encouragement to them to keep at it - it should not be allowed.

'The General Election (held in July 1945) was the main topic of conversation and I remember the local MP promising to have The Leas shut and the men moved elsewhere if he was voted in. Clem Attlee became the new Labour Prime Minister and that was the end of that. All we were interested in was an end to the war.

'In the physiotherapy department I had to attend every second day were a few Polish WAAFs. Their language was impossible to understand so there was little conversation. It was decided that three of us who were not making any progress with kneebending should attend a civilian hospital in Liverpool. This was early May 1945.

'Our chief medical officer, Squadron Leader Cantor, explained the scenario. 'It's only for a day - next Friday in fact,' he said. 'The idea is for you chaps to receive deep penetration X-rays that we hope will yield results. The idea is for it to break down the lesions which are the result of having your legs in plaster for so long.

'I have learned from the hospital that results have been encouraging and should help you chaps. Oh, as it's on Friday you chaps will not be able to go on 48-hour pass this weekend as the treatment could cause pain in the knee area after about 24 hours.' (Cantor was very fond of the words 'you chaps.') He added: 'So we think you should remain here just in case.'

'As soon as he had finished, McDermott, the Australian, informed the MO that he had to attend a wedding at which he was best man. I quickly added that I was expected in Sheffield as I was to become engaged to a nurse. If I were to experience any great discomfort, she would make sure I was taken care of at the local hospital where I had been a patient before coming to The Leas. Both of us were telling lies, but not to be able to travel to Sheffield was unbearable in my case. There was silence; I stared at the MO, more lies queuing up behind my teeth. I can still see him, sitting in his chair, hands clasped, leaning forward with a disarming smile saying, 'You chaps will have to do better than that!'

Mac gave a troubled frown and then asked if we could check with the MO on Saturday morning. 'If we have no pain, can we go?' He agreed. We were taken to Liverpool by van , visited the X-ray department and were cleared to leave the hospital just before noon, all feeling hungry as we had missed our morning break. The driver was told to take us via Chinatown to visit a small cafe, run by Chinese, where we could have eggs and bacon with tinned tomatoes and white bread. The bread itself was worth the trip, after the rather grey wartime bread. It was, we thought, either purloined from US ships or made from flour which had somehow turned up white by mistake in the Chinese cafe.

'In December 1945 I was discharged from the RAF Hospital at Halton, Buckinghamshire, and sent to another rehabilitation centre at Chessington in Surrey, not far from my home. I was finally invalided out of the RAF in August 1946 after two years in hospitals and various other postings round the country.'

In a letter to the author, Frank Munro added these comments: 'I think for many of my fellow airmen the war was the most exciting event of our lives, for we were actually making history. It was a unique experience. Others - those young people who have been spared the experience of war - fail to understand this.'

A Wartime Haven

RAY SMITH, a former Royal New Zealand Air Force Sergeant Pilot, service number 41951, who returned to New Zealand after the war, remembers The Leas well. His letter to the author in February 2001 contained the photographs reproduced in this appendix and the following memories and reflections.

Patients at The Leas relaxing on camp stools. The prefab building (in the trees) formed part of the sleeping quarters.
(Photo via Ray Smith)

Extreme left, Ray Smith. Next to him, Barney Brumby. The patients are sunbathing beside the strong back wall built to convert the fives court for the game of squash.
(Photo via Ray Smith)

121

'Mention of this wartime haven for broken aircrew bodies certainly brought back many cherished memories associated with that rehabilitation centre. Looking through the few mementoes I collected during the short time (July-November 1942) spent at The Leas stirs up feelings of deep emotion, remembering the comradeship and freedom from stress pervading that home. But, alas, a flood of sadness inevitably follows. Being reminded of the wonderful mates whose lives were cut short soon after returning to their respective bases leaves a cavernous hole in one's gut.

'I turned 21 while at The Leas and am facing my 80th year now but have not completely got over the sadness of those losses. Obviously, I survived and my life since has been filled with the fun of living, just as theirs should have been following on from their demobilisation. For me, being a patient at The Leas at the right time finally led to my future happiness. Two New Zealanders were required to fill an invitation to spend a weekend with an appreciative family in Lymm, Cheshire. Don Harkness and myself were the lucky Kiwis named by the adjutant.

'We had a wonderful time and were asked to return some time. I did just that whenever the opportunity arose. Thanks to that kind family, I met the girl who, years later, was to become my lifelong partner. Don did not make it back to New Zealand. Nor did a wonderful friend, Barney Brumby who, together with me and a Canadian, Dovey, formed a trio seldom seen separated on any outing from The Leas.'

Flying Days Over

FLIGHT SGT RON GILL, Wireless Operator/Air Gunner, arrived at The Leas in January 1942. He had just spent three months in hospital with severe injuries as the result of a bad crash in East Anglia. He was flying in a Wellington returning from bombing Frankfurt. He spent six weeks at The Leas and recalls that there were still notices on the wall indicating its former use as a private boarding school for boys. (Author's Note - It was used again as a school after the war until its closure. The Leas was eventually pulled down and houses built on the site.)

'While there, I was given exercises daily, mainly to strengthen my back and I also had to play Fives each day. There was an interesting collection of aircrew and we were treated very well. Occasionally a member of the Press would telephone to ask if there were any interesting casualties that they could report on in the papers.

'We were allowed out in the evenings and among the various local pubs we visited were The Ship in Hoylake and The Dee Hotel in West Kirby. I also remember myself and another patient spending a weekend in Chester during the later stages of our treatment. When I left The Leas, my flying days were over and I was grounded for the rest of the war. Little did I think that in the years ahead, I would living so near to The Leas - at Meols.'

The Leas.
(Photo via Ray Smith)

The Flying Enterprise

SIX weeks before the author completed his two years National Service, the drama of the Flying Enterprise, adrift in storms off Cornwall, began. For ten days, the story made front page news and buzzed around HQ Coastal Command as the author began his countdown to demob. Aircraft from two Coastal Command airfields, St Eval and St Mawgan, overflew the ship and photographers fortunate enough to be carried on them, obtained dramatic pictures of the brave captain waving from the deck of his stricken ship. Peter Hardyman has sent the author an extract from his father's log book recording that he flew over the Flying Enterprise as navigator in a Lancaster MR (Maritime Reconnaissance) III of 210 Squadron from St Eval on January 3, 1952.

The Flying Enterprise.
(Copyright photo, Mirror Group Newspapers)

On board were photographers from the Daily Express, Daily Herald, Daily Mirror, BBC News and Gaumont-British News. Gaumont-British News was one of the three organisations supplying newsreels to the cinemas; the others were Pathe and British Movietone. Flight Lieutenant Hardyman had been posted to St Eval on June 13, 1951. His service number was 165368, Christian names Richard James Trenchard.

Brian Buswell, a 'sprog' Flying Officer pilot newly transferred from Transport Command for the rapid expansion of Coastal Command, was attending No 8 Maritime Reconnaissance Course at St Mawgan at the time. Coastal Command was being expanded because of the Russian submarine threat. He lived in the Trelawney Hotel, Newquay, from December 14, 1951, until March 7, 1952.

'Conditions at St Mawgan (which had reopened the previous Spring) were rugged, to say the least, with people scattered around in temporary accommodation and working from leaking huts and messes. How the ground crews kept the Lancasters serviceable was miraculous,' Brian stated. 'The Lancasters kept a close watch on the Flying Enterprise. The episode would have been controlled from the Rescue Coordination Centre at No 19 Group Headquarters at Plymouth. ' (Staff captains on the Maritime Reconnaissance School and some of the Lancasters remembered by Brian Buswell are listed at the end of this Appendix).

SGT STEVE VESSEY was also undergoing maritime conversion at St Mawgan and made two trips to the Flying Enterprise in January 1952. The first was on January 2, in Lancaster MRIII SW284 with Sgt Horn as pilot. It was an operational flying exercise to locate and photograph the vessel. Steve records: 'My memory is that the weather was not very good, but we found the ship without difficulty and flew round until the photographer had got all the pictures he wanted before returning to base.'

His second flight was on January 9 in Lancaster MRIII RE322, pilot, Flight Sgt Stastny. This was a radar exercise to locate the Flying Enterprise. 'The weather on this occasion was dreadful with a gale blowing, 8/8 stratus (continuous cloud) at 1000 feet and very poor visibility. Although we found the ship without any problem, our pilot deemed that it was too dangerous to remain in the area, since a number of private aircraft carrying Press reporters and photographers were orbiting the vessel and there was a serious risk of collision.'

Steve was a newly-trained air gunner, being converted to radar gunner, i.e. radar operator and general factotum on Coastal Command. He enjoyed radar and carried out the homing on January 9, having been taken to roughly the right place by the pilot and navigator. He tried to get photographs of the ship that day, but failed because they did not get close enough due to the weather and other aircraft. Steve was a National Serviceman. Although it was normally difficult for a National Serviceman

125

to be selected for aircrew, at this time it was easier because the RAF had introduced two large-crew aircraft - the Washington (B29) and the Shackleton - and many wartime aircrew had left the Service. The Shackleton, for instance, carried a crew of ten.

The Flying Enterprise, a former liberty ship of 6711 gross tons, belonged to the Isbrantdsen Line. Her captain, the Danish-born Kurt Carlsen, was from New Jersey. The ship left Hamburg just before Christmas Day 1951, bound for New York and on Boxing Day ran into a Force 12 hurricane off the Cornish coast, described as the worst for 75 years. A 60-feet sea hit the ship broadside and sheared off the rudder. It also knocked the cargo to one side and the ship started listing.

The owners told Carlsen he could leave the ship but he decided to stay. On December 29 Carlsen ordered the 45 members of the crew and the ten passengers to jump into the sea to be picked up by other ships which had been called by radio. For six days and nights, he was alone on the ship.

On January 2, the British rescue tug Turmoil, 1136 tons, commanded by Captain D. Parker, left Falmouth to attempt to tow the Flying Enterprise into that port, reaching the vessel next day. Seven attempts were made to get a towline on board but, because of the ship's angle and its lurching in the heavy swell, Carlsen could not make the line fast. Kenneth Dancy, first mate of the Turmoil, succeeded on January 4 in jumping from the tug to the ship and the following day the towline was connected.

Towing continued for the next four days but when only 57 miles from Falmouth, tug and tow were forced to heave to by heavy storms. Next day, the towline parted and, after drifting in heavy swell, the Flying Enterprise sank on January 10. Carlsen and Dancy jumped into the water 40 minutes before she sank and were picked up five minutes later by the Turmoil. A helicopter rescue was considered on the afternoon of January 10 but the helicopter was forced to return to its base at Culdrose because of the severe weather.

Brian Buswell adds the comment that helicopters were fairly new at that time, were temperamental and rescue procedures were primitive by today's standards.

Files in the Post Office Archive record that Land's End radio station was the main link between shore and the drama being played out at sea. The RSGB Bulletin for February 1952 'regretted that so little recognition was given by the Press to the magnificent job done by the GPO operators in handling many hundreds of messages each day in addition to their normal traffic.'

For his courage, Carlsen received the Lloyds medal because his action had meant another shipping company could not claim the Flying Enterprise for salvage; a Danish knighthood from King Frederick and merchant marine medals from Belgium, France and Morocco. In London, he received the Order of Daneborg at the Danish Club in Knightsbridge; the crowds outside were shouting 'We want Carlsen,' and called out 'Bravo' and 'Well done, Carlsen' when he appeared at a window.

The above account of the saga was compiled from Keasing's Contemporary Archives, the files of the Eastern Daily Press and a story published in the Daily Telegraph for October 11, 1989, reporting Captain Carlsen's death. The Telegraph account states that mystery had always surrounded the £600,000 cargo of the Flying Enterprise which was said to have included coffee, iron, antiques and even zirconium for the first American nuclear submarine. In the same report, Carlsen is quoted as saying that there was a lot of money in the ship's holds, being sent in dollars and pound notes from a Swiss bank to a bank in the US. It had been sent by ordinary mail, which was illegal. He believed that it was eventually salvaged and dried out in the kitchen below a bank in Belgium.

A report in the Western Morning News on January 11, 1952, gave a graphic account of the final stages of the sinking. It states: 'But as the storms worsened, the Enterprise, her tow rope snapped, was rolling so badly that her superstructure barely showed above the waves. Then, frightfully, her stern plummeted, her bows pointed skywards... and just 39 minutes before she succumbed to the ocean, Carlsen and Dancy hauled themselves up the funnel and jumped into the raging water, hauntingly lit by the flares which had fallen from the decks. The two men were picked up minutes later by Turmoil.

'An officer of the US destroyer, Willard Keith, which had been escorting the Enterprise, reports the ship's demise over the radio-telephone: 'It was an eerie sight in the deepening gloom...suddenly, she plunged stern first, and only that tell-tale swirl, which many of our men saw in the Pacific war, remained."

Reminiscences of Arthur Charles 'Toby' West, published in the Western Morning News in 1999, recall that the Falmouth lifeboat was launched but was unable to get to the Enterprise before it sank and was recalled to the station. Toby West, who spent nearly 40 years on Falmouth's lifeboats, wrote: 'At the time, there was much mystery concerning this ship. My brother and myself were paid £5 each plus all the beer we could drink, supposedly discussing all the mystery at the pub, the Chain Locker in Falmouth, in the presence of the many reporters who had been waiting in Falmouth for her arrival.'

In May 2000, the same newspaper recalled that the lifeboat from Cadgwith Cove in Cornwall, the Dunkirk Guide, was also called to the assistance of the Flying Enterprise.' The Guide of Dunkirk, originally intended to be the Clacton lifeboat, received her name for her part in the rescue of British troops from the Dunkirk beaches in 1940. Renamed Girl Guide, she was still a tourist attraction in 2000.

Staff captains at the Maritime Reconnaissance School recalled by Brian Buswell: Sgt Hunt, Flight Sgt Nast, Flight Lieutenant Walker, Flying Officer Delany, Master Pilot Sneller, Flight Lieutenant Kozlowski, Sgt Worthing, Flight Sgt Bishop, Sgt Edwards, Sgt Davis. Some of the Lancasters at the School at that time were: RE 159, PB 529, RE 287, SW 366, RF 327, PB 965, SW 328, RF 303.

Appendix V

National Service in the Postwar Period

National Service was a fact of life for most medically-fit young men who reached the age of 18 between 1948 and 1960. They completed a period of full-time military service - for most it was two years - followed by a period on the reserve when they could be recalled if the country needed them. If you were a miner, a farmworker or a minister of religion, you were exempt from the call-up. A few people registered as conscientious objectors and worked full-time in the hospital service as an alternative.

Men had continued to be called up for military service after World War II to meet the country's commitments to its dwindling Empire, to provide an Army of occupation, with frontline air support from the RAF, in Germany and to have forces available for any other emergencies. Ever present was the shadow of the Cold War - the threat posed by the USSR (Russia) who were now masters of Eastern Europe.

Passing out parade, with parents present.

129

The National Service Act, introduced in July 1947, provided for one year's full-time military service. But, from 1948, the Army faced commitments much larger than expected, so the full-time period was increased - first to 18 months and then, with the outbreak of the Korean War in 1950, to two years. There was a sweetener for those who did the two years after 1950. For the final six months' service, they received the same rate of pay as regulars. (Author's Note: In my case, an extra three shillings (15p) a day, bringing my pay to 11 shillings (55p) a day.) The extra pay was tempting to many who signed on for three years at the start of their service and were often selected for the trade of their choice.

National Service was unpopular with many recruits. Even their mothers complained. An article by Arthur Eperon in the Daily Herald, reprinted in the Royal Air Force Review in June 1949, attempted to answer some of these complaints. The article began: 'You can rarely pick up a magazine these days without seeing a letter from an irate mother complaining that her son is wasting 18 months in the Services when he ought to be learning a job, or a letter from an anonymous serviceman hinting that he has spent most of his 18 months lying on his bunk studying the ceiling of the hut.'

'Men of my generation,' Arthur Eperon wrote, 'whose careers were postponed for six years from 1939 to 1945, read the letters from the irate parents with tolerant amusement. We read the letters from the idle servicemen with considerable envy.'

He quoted from his own experience. 'In my crew in 1941 was a flight engineer named Jock. Jock did not have much time even to sleep. He flew at night and worked on the aircraft during the day. But Jock wanted to matriculate (pass the examination necessary for university entrance). So he used to study Latin over the North Sea on the way back from a raid. His studying was a gamble because he had only a fifty-fifty chance of living to take the examination. He was killed before he could take it.'

The article also mentions a woman complaining that her son had failed to get his military service deferred and had had to postpone his university entrance. She thought he might have lost interest in going to university after 18 months in the Air Force. Arthur Eperon commented: 'All I can say is that if he could lose interest so quickly, it would have been a waste of time to send him anyway. My contemporaries who went to university had their entrance deferred by six years. But I never heard them complain.'

If some National Servicemen spent time lying on their beds, others fought in postwar hotspots like Malaya, Korea, Aden, Kenya, Cyprus and Suez. In all, nearly 400 National Servicemen were killed on active service. The Defence White Paper of 1957 envisaged the use of nuclear weapons as the main deterrent to any expansion plans by the USSR in Europe. The use of tactical nuclear weapons could cut manpower needs. Large numbers of transport aircraft and helicopters would give the Army the flexibility it needed and so bring an end to National Service.

Volunteers would provide an Army, Navy and Air Force of the size required - a cut from 690,000 to 375,000 by the end of 1962, when the last National Serviceman was due to leave the Forces.

The last intake of the two million National Servicemen were called up in November 1960 and they served for 2½ years to allow the build-up of regulars to be achieved. The last National Serviceman to leave the RAF was said to have been SAC Joe Wallace, on January 23, 1963. In all 433,087 National Servicemen were recruited to the RAF (Source: Stand By Yer Beds). Of the 155,000 recruits trained at West Kirby between 1946 and 1957, the majority were National Servicemen.

The debate still goes on as to the value of National Service to the individual. The writer Alan Bennett, not primarily a military man, wrote this in the London Review of Books on January 25, 2001: 'Part of the pleasure I had in National Service was that it represented delayed schooling, and that for the first time I was away from home. No politician would dare suggest it, but six months or a year of National Service nowadays, provided the time was well used, would seem to me to do little harm and have many advantages.'

The RAF was keen to get National Servicemen to sign on for three years or more, hence this display of trades open to regulars.

Bibliography

RAF Coastal Command 1936-1969. By Chris Ashworth (Patrick Stephens)

An Erk's Eye View. By Ted Caton

The Fort on the Hill, The Story of Royal Air Force Hereford. By Terrence J. Knight

Brasso Blanco and Bull, By Tony Thorne. (Rogerson Press)

Stand By Yer Beds. By John F. Hamlin (GMS Enterprises)

Fire by Night. By Jennie Gray (Grub Street)

The People's War. By Angus Calder (Granada)

Glossary

Ablutions - Washroom

Airman - The term applied to personnel below the rank of corporal - the RAF equivalent of soldier

Anklets - Short gaiters, worn with boots during basic training

AOA - Air Officer Administration

AOC - Air Officer Commanding

AOC-in-C - Air Officer Commanding-in-Chief

ATC - Air Training Corps

Battledress - Working dress (blouse-type tunic and trousers)

Bed Card - Card placed above an individual's bed listing number, rank, name, trade and religion

Bedspace - The area round an individual's bed which he or she was responsible for keeping clean

Best blue - No 1 service dress (brass-buttoned tunic, trousers and 'best' hat or cap)

Billet - Alternative for barrack room or hut but also used for accommodation off camp

Blighty - Slang for Britain

Bull - Slang for over-intensive cleaning, polishing and blancoing demanded during basic training. Also used for anything considered irrelevant, e.g 'load of old bull'

Bullnight - Slang for domestic night when the hut, barrack room, ablutions etc, had to be cleaned thoroughly. It was usual to be confined to camp for that evening

Civvies - Civilian clothes or civilians

Civvy Street - Civilian life

Demob (demobilisation) - Release from full-time service in the Forces

DPs (Displaced Persons) - People from European countries who came to Britain as refugees at the end of World War II

ENSA - Entertainments National Service Association. This agency was set up to provide entertainment for the services at home and abroad and to industry during World War II. Its director was the distinguished theatrical producer, Basil Dean. By early 1946, ENSA had given over 2½ million concerts. Though it attracted some stars, ENSA relied heavily on low-grade and near-amateur talent, hence its nickname 'Every Night Something Awful.' (Source: The People's War)

Erk - Recruit

Fatigues - Routine cookhouse, cleaning or other duties. Recruits normally did one week of fatigues. Fatigues could also be awarded as a punishment

GD - General Duties

Grounded - Removed from flying duties

HQ - Headquarters

Irons - Knife, fork and spoon

Jankers - Slang for confined to camp as a punishment. It involved reporting to the guardoom several times a day in full kit - haversack, belt, etc

Kit - Uniform and equipment issued to the recruit on joining. Used more generally to describe the equipment, vehicles etc used by the Service

Kitbag - The circular canvas bag, about three feet high, in which kit is packed when moving to another station

Kit inspection - The ritual (and detailed) inspection of an individual's kit, by an NCO or officer. The kit had to be laid out on the bed to a strict pattern

Mess - Dining hall

MR - Maritime Reconnaissance

MT - Motor Transport

NAAFI - Navy, Army and Air Force Institutes. The organisation best known among recruits for providing canteens at Service establishments

NCO - Non-commissioned Officer. The ranks of Corporal, Sergeant, Flight Sergeant and Warrant Officer

OC - Officer Commanding

Pass - Permit to be off camp for a fixed period, e.g. 48 hours

Passing out - The final parade at the end of basic training

PDC - Personnel Dispatch Centre, often called transit camp

PSI - President of the Service Institute. This was the title taken by the officer, or sometimes a civilian, presiding over the committee which administered the PSI fund. The messes and the NAAFI contributed to this fund. The committee met six-monthly and considered applications for grants to buy items like radios for the billets or other welfare items

PT - Physical Training

PTI - Physical Training Instructor

Ranks - **AC2** - Aircraftman Second Class
AC1 - Aircraftman First Class
LAC - Leading Aircraftman
SAC - Senior Aircraftman
Cpl - Corporal
Sgt - Sergeant
Flight Sgt - Flight Sergeant
WO - Warrant Officer
(In this book, officers' ranks are given in full, e.g. Flight Lieutenant)

Remuster - Change trade

Regular - A volunteer who signs on for a fixed-term of years in any of the Services

Reserve service - The period after demobilisation when the individual is liable for recall, e.g. in the case of a national emergency

Rooky - Recruit

SP - Service Police, i.e. the RAF's police service

SIB - Special Investigation Branch - senior members of the RAF police service, called in to investigate serious crimes. They wore civilian clothes

Sprog - A beginner. Often used of someone in the early stages of being transferred from training to a permanent station

Station - An RAF location, e.g. airfield, Maintenance Unit, recruit centre etc

Square - Parade ground

Squarebashing - Initial training

SWO (or SWO man) - Station Warrant Officer

Tannoy - Public address system

VAD - Voluntary Aid Detachment. Volunteers enrolled via the British Red Cross Society and St John Ambulance Brigade who served in Service hospitals. They assisted in many roles in addition to nursing duties

Webbing - Canvas belt, straps, packs (large and small haversacks) and anklets

1250 - RAF identity card